Don't Pick Up the Bill

Strategies to Help Affluent Individuals & Families Navigate a New Economic & Tax Paradigm

By

Ronald M. Roth

ISBN: 978-1-949565-72-0

Contents

Dedication

For Claudia, Zachary & Hanna….my reason for reason, always.

ACKNOWLEDGEMENTS

A project such as this is always a team effort. I want to begin by thanking my partners Joe Tucciarone and Anita Bryant. When I first met Joe and Anita almost 25 years ago, I was taken by their intelligence, focus, and visionary approach to our industry. Although we didn't reconnect in business until three years ago, Claudia and I consider ourselves quite lucky to be partnering with Joe and Anita and appreciate their never ending confidence and love.

I would also like to thank and recognize the entire team at National Network of Accountants. This organization in in essence a family business. Even given our aggressive national growth model, we will always at heart be a family business and look forward to welcoming new associates and clients into this wonder family. The first person I met at NNA was Pamela Romano. From day one, she made me feel like I belonged here and over the years has had confidence in my vision and has become like a sister to me. The first person in our office every morning is Joseph Tucciarone, Jr. I appreciate his consistency, honesty, and Joe Jr. is someone who I would want next to me in any battle. To Kathy Caridi who knows every aspect of our business and keeps the NNA train on track. To Marc Scharf who is always my sounding board for financial strategies and my favorite associate to be in the field with. To Paul Hyl, Esq for his help reviewing and fine-tuning Chapter 8 and for consistently "dotting all the I's, crossing all the T's", and always making us look smart. To Susan Lauletta who makes it easy for me to write for NNA because she is such a good editor. To Larry Posen for his relentless drive and enthusiasm. To Dave Goldberg who made a large contribution to this book by helping me crystalize "CIC" and the importance it represents to the top one percent. Finally, to my friend Cathy Bianculli who is responsible for helping keep our business operating smoothly and efficiently financially.

I would also like to thank our team in Israel who is helping expand and grow our business both at home and abroad. To Fran, Sol, Barry, Dikla, and Shoshana at Sunhouse Marketing for their creativity and dedication to our brand.

To Ken Small and his team for making this manuscript become a reality and their ongoing support and patience in the process.

To Maria and Melissa at Lifetime for helping me to rediscover my inner strength and find my peace. They have been an integral part of one of the most rewarding journeys of my life.

To Gilda and Tony Spataro for their love and support always. I have known Tony to be one of the strongest people I have ever met and this year he has shown us that strength and resilience.

To Barry and Gary Roth who have been by my side this most challenging year for our family. Our Geri would be reminding us to count our blessings and of those we are lucky to have so many.

Most importantly to Claudia, Zachary, and Hanna ... thank you for your confidence, love, and support in everything I do. None of it would make any sense without the three of you.

Introduction

Are you an affluent individual that endeavors to grow, protect, and preserve your wealth and assets while saving large amounts of money for yourself, your business, your family, and ultimately your heirs? That's what I was hoping you would say! My goal throughout this book is to offer strategies and information that can help you to achieve victories in these areas. Because you plucked this book off the shelf or added it to your online shopping cart and waited (with bated breath, I hope) for it to arrive on your doorstep, I am going to assume that you have a thriving business or professional practice that you've poured your energy, determination, and a lot of hard work into.

Consider your beginnings, how your life changed greatly after you finished school and you accepted your first position on the bottom rung on your projected career ladder, started a business from scratch, or maybe you were the newbie in an established family business. Back then, everything you owned may well have fit into your car. Then things began to change as your business or practice grew, and you started to accumulate wealth and significant assets. Now you will do anything you can to guard and protect them, not just for yourself, but for your children, grandchildren, and even for future generations. Or perhaps the pandemic reinforced the idea that life hangs by a slender thread that may give way at any moment, so you need to be prepared for all eventualities. Missed opportunities to save large amounts of money (especially on taxes) can occur without proper preparation and knowledge. What can you do? What plans can you implement to safeguard your estate… your wealth… your assets? What measures will you need to allow it to grow? How do you retain as much control as possible regarding how your estate will be disbursed to your heirs?

This book is exactly what you need to navigate these changing times. In it, I will share with you some of the knowledge I've gained over the more than thirty years that I've been working on these very issues for high-net-worth individuals and families. I've helped people just like you to preserve, protect, and grow their estates and wealth. If you're one of the many who daydream about what your future holds, are someone who harbours a multitude of desires for the future of your business/professional endeavours, and you even wish for a roadmap for your heirs so they can carry everything forward with greater diligence, it's time to replace that word *wish* with a solid plan. Eleanor Roosevelt once noted that "[i] t takes as much energy to wish as it does to plan."

While some of you may have been fortunate enough to have inherited a thriving family business, others of you had to channel your entrepreneurial efforts to build your business from the ground up. Or maybe you established a professional practice by putting in long hours dedicating yourself to gain the trust of your community by building a reputation for excellence. Whether your wealth was the result of keeping your eye on your goal, working zealously, and striving to always be the best, or if it was by maintaining and expanding an inherited and well-established business or practice, your wealth did not appear on your doorstep like that fifth Amazon package of the week that you completely forgot you ordered. And unlike your average Amazon order which can be easily placed and just as easily replaced if lost or mislaid, it is no easy feat to build and then hold onto true wealth, whether acquired by dint of relentless drive and applying shrewd business acumen, or by cultivating and expanding inherited wealth. You took risks, recognized opportunities, set your plans in motion, and reaped your well-deserved rewards. As you built, expanded, and nurtured your business, you made sacrifices. You no doubt spent long hours focused on your business. You may have had to travel frequently which meant that you missed spending time with loved ones. You worked hard and made those sacrifices to build a flourishing business or professional practice and to accumulate the wealth and assets that have provided you with the sort of financial security that brings a measure of freedom.

With the accumulation of wealth and assets, and the establishment of a thriving business or professional endeavor, comes a strong desire to protect and preserve and grow what you have worked so hard to establish and build. In feudal England, you would have had your overflowing coffers of gold, silver, and gems secured in a strong room with posted guards outside. If possible, you would have raised the drawbridge. That's sort of the medieval equivalent of stuffing your banknotes in your mattress, but with cool things like moats, drawbridges, and maybe even crenelated walls. (Side note: Did you know that because of the advantage they gave in a battle or a siege, a person couldn't add crenelated walls to his castle without the permission of the monarch?) I read of a ninety-year-old man whose parents had instilled in him a distrust of banks because of what they and their families had suffered during the Great Depression. Poor guy had always kept his money at home, but when his family employed a caregiver to spend the day with him, the old man took to carrying his money around in a bag…a brown paper bag. He left it in a drugstore one day, but was exceedingly lucky that someone found it, saw his name inside, and got it back to him. Whew! Still, I shudder to think of how that money could have worked for him. There are countless missed opportunities he could have utilized to increase his net worth had he not stashed it in a paper bag. Your money isn't going to achieve all that it could if it's tucked away in a bag or wrapped up in an inefficient or outdated investment strategy. Today, you need sophisticated and meticulous planning to keep your wealth and assets safe and growing.

Your priorities and what you devote most (if not all) of your professional attention to will shift as you move along the path of your life. Early in your career, you were likely focused on building and growing your business and your wealth. Now as you move along in life, you should begin to consider how best to retain the assets and wealth you have accumulated and grown through assiduous attention and meticulous care over the course of your lifetime.

As you grow older and perhaps have children and eventually grandchildren, your priorities will change. Naturally, you will start to think of your legacy, what you will leave behind to your family, and who will take over the business or professional practice you have built from the ground up. Or, if none of the preceding options seem appealing, you could always leave your estate to your trusted financial advisor. But in all seriousness, your focused efforts have been and will continue to be an investment in your dream for your future, your desire to succeed no matter how steep the climb to the top. Still more than that, it is an investment in your legacy, a testament to the fulfilment of the plans you made as you embarked on your career. It will not only be a parting gift for the people you love, but also a lasting memorial to the plans you made, to your drive and determination to make those plans a reality, and to the business or practice that you built and maintained.

For those of you in the earlier stages of your careers, you are focused on establishing your business or professional practice and amassing your wealth; your goals are different from those of us in the later stage of our lives. While not quite at the stage where you have begun thinking of what you will leave behind, to whom you will leave it, and how much you will give, you undoubtedly are working toward that very stage even if you aren't aware of it or are executing formal plans to structure your wishes. To make it to the top 1 percent requires tenacity, but once you are there, staying there is no walk in the park. However, if you are reading this book, then chances are that despite your age, you are either already within that 1 percent or well on your way. In either scenario, kudos are in order.

Regardless of your age or how much you intend to earn or you have earned thus far, one fact of life rings true for us all: the only constant in life is change. Ignorance of the changes happening in the world around you could be detrimental to both your personal and your business interests. In this book, my goal is to educate you on the changes that are inevitably coming to our tax system which will affect your wealth. I will bring to your attention pertinent changes to federal law, specifically the tax code, which have the potential to negatively affect your holdings. I will also point out and discuss changes in the tax code that are under discussion on Capitol Hill or are in the works to be added to the tax code. My aim is to help you to recognize where these changes might affect your holdings, and then to mitigate any potential mistakes that otherwise might result in a loss of your hard-earned wealth.

Plain and Simple

Like many of you, I am of the opinion that the emergence of high net worth is not something that occurs by chance or divine intervention. Very few people stumble into a fortune. Yes, there are a fortunate few who win their millions in a lottery. I find it interesting that statistics show that most of those individuals are bankrupt within eight years of receiving the prize. That statistic illustrates that even when someone is gifted or inherits large amounts of money, that person must rise up and take charge of their money by investing and sheltering it-or they will face losing the entire sum no matter how vast.

It takes a combination of commendable resolve, business intuitiveness, patience, and time to build a profitable business and accumulate wealth/assets. Once built or inherited, wealth requires an equal amount of savvy and persistent attention to maintain and grow. Ignore that fact and you'll lose what you worked so diligently to build.

If you do a bit of research, you'll find that when an individual founds a business, takes it to the top of its sector, and accumulates a fortune, in most cases the fortune is gone by the third generation. The business may be guided by individuals who are not part of the founder's family. You may wonder how this could happen. Businesses such as these no doubt had humble beginnings but grew into very large enterprises that became well known and fantastically successful. The individual who founded the business and devoted themselves to making it a success, was driven, ambitious, and sacrificed endlessly to ensure its prosperity. Sadly, even if the founder makes provisions so that a family member can assume the helm of the business to nurture and maintain it, continuing the founder's work and preparing the business for the future does not always happen. The founder may die suddenly before making plans for the business's future, or the individual in the next generation who was tapped to lead the business forward, lacks the drive, determination, and business knowledge to do the job properly. Some people would rather spend the business's money than spend time working. This leads to a third generation — the grandchildren of the founders — who are happy to consume the rewards generated by their predecessor but are completely removed from the operation of the business. They may turn the day-to-day control over to outsiders who know next to nothing about what is happening with the business or its market sector. That's a scary scenario to contemplate, isn't it? You can't build a business, accumulate wealth and assets, and then cease to look after it; you'll lose it. Of course, it doesn't have to go that way if the business creator puts solid plans in place to control and guide the future of their business long after they have passed on.

With the hard work and determination, it takes to generate a substantial estate, one might think that you would be able to keep your accumulative wealth intact and distribute it as you pleased when you pleased. Well, thanks to tax laws and regulations, that's not necessarily the way things will go unless you take steps through careful planning to ensure that your will prevails. Now, as I am sure you are all acutely aware, taxes do not seem to be going down any time soon. The late comedian, Broadway actor, and astute student of human nature who was also known as Oklahoma's favorite son, Will Rogers, had this to say regarding taxes: "The only difference between death and taxes is that death doesn't get worse every time Congress meets." He was right. New legislation only serves to increase the labyrinthine convolutions of the tax code. There are provisions in that code that can really help you, but you really need to know where to find them. There are also provisions in the code that can have devastating ramifications for you and your holdings if you misconstrue or are unaware of them.

Compounding the difficulty of sheltering your assets and income from taxation is the increasingly popular belief held by many Americans that some people simply have too much wealth while others have too little. From that belief, a notion has evolved that those with the most wealth and assets need to give up a greater portion of their assets through taxation to help others. Because the country's economy, budget deficits, and national debt are stressed to extreme limits, some legislators have succumbed to popular demand and argue that substantial amounts of your wealth should be redistributed to other Americans through some form of wealth tax or other confiscatory taxes. That could mean imposing a higher taxation rate on people with a determined net worth or levying a tax that would effectively take a percentage of a high-net- worth individual's wealth. Taxes and the laws enforcing them are fickle by nature, perhaps even more so than the promises from a campaigning politician's lips. However, a growing call to levy heavy taxes on the rich has been rumbling among some Americans for years. If you consider the fact that the most significant wealth transfer in history (from the Baby Boomers to their children) has already begun to take place, this is a good time for Congress to grab some of that money as it changes hands. Remember: forewarned is forearmed *if* you take steps to plan and protect your wealth.

The idea of losing a large percentage of the holdings that you worked so hard to accrue isn't a welcoming concept. Your business reached its position of profitability because you controlled its development, not because you allowed outsiders to determine its course and how its revenue would be invested and spent. Because of that, I would expect the idea that someone intervening and grabbing some of your profits to use for projects of their creation — that *they* deem important — would rankle you. When you donate to a charity, I would expect you to thoroughly investigate that charity to ensure that your donation would be used according to the charity's stated purpose and your expectation. You wouldn't hand over money to provide relief for the victims of a natural disaster only to find out that the charitable entity intended to buy new carpeting for its headquarters. You would likely give a grandchild pocket money to spend as they wished without strings, but in other situations, you would want to control how your money was spent. What will happen after your death, when you're not here to keep track of how the wealth you strived and sacrificed to achieve is being used?

Envision a scenario where large amounts of your hard-earned wealth disappear when you die, with those assets not going to your children, grandchildren, or other heirs, but rather to the government to be redistributed to whomever or whatever the government deems as deserving of a subsidy. I will resist the temptation to point out the numerous incidents where the government spent tax dollars inefficiently and ineptly. Quite frankly, I do not have the time nor the temperament, and I doubt there's enough paper on hand to record them all. This is a book on wealth strategies and planning, so this is where I will concentrate my efforts. However, I will point out that every day, this ill-conceived notion of extra taxes on the top 1 percent drifts further from an adventitious problem for our future selves to more of a grim sneak peek of what is likely to come. Yes, I believe it is time to take a hard look at this problem and make plans to mitigate the setbacks it could cause you.

Regardless of where you land politically, I think we can all agree that suitable investments should yield greater returns than bad investments, and hard work, commitment, and success should be rewarded and not penalized with the addition of excess taxation. Though I suppose if we did not share these commonalities, you would not be reading this book, now would you?

Success Should Be Rewarded

Our capitalist economy may not be perfect, but there is no denying that it has allowed more people to raise themselves out of poverty or limited means than any other economic system in history. Because of capitalism and the opportunities, it presents, multitudes of Americans have been able to pursue business endeavors and accumulate wealth that would have astounded their forefathers. A large part of the allure and promise of capitalism is the freedom it affords. If an individual has a solid plan for an endeavour and works hard, that individual can reach the top of their business and the top 1 percent of wealth holders. Whether an individual fails or succeeds is largely up to that individual's determination and efforts. Through hard work and good business sense, an individual can accumulate wealth. Then, the astute move is to enlist the help of a competent advisor to ensure that the individual's wealth and assets are preserved and grow during their lifetime. Although no one can take their wealth and assets with them when they pass on, by putting in place meticulous plans, they can ensure that their estate is handed down to their next generations in the manner they stipulated.

I liken this to having dinner out with my family or close friends. I love their company and the memorable conversations that complement the experience in the way a fine wine adds to a gourmet meal. I will often gladly pick up the tab for family, close friends, and business colleagues. I truly relish those experiences. How many vivid memories do you have that involve good company and superior food? On a few occasions, I have picked up the tab for a stranger as well, but I treasure treating those I love to a good meal. I don't mind if it's five-star cuisine at an upscale eatery or a greasy hamburger at my favorite dive bar; I enjoy the experience, the company, and the jolly times. Yet the thing that makes these acts truly gratifying to me is that I do them at *my* discretion and not because someone commanded that I pick up the bill.

However, what gives otherwise good food a poor taste in my mouth is the unwarranted expansion of my guest list — without my permission — to include people I have never met and with whom I will never become acquainted. If you have yet to pick up on the analogy, this is what the government is thinking of doing, but without the delicious food. They are creating an extensive bill for large government expenditures which include things like expanded unemployment benefits and recurring stimulus payments among many other things. The caveat to this is they will be presenting *us* with the bill.

Incompetent government spending (a tautological statement indeed) combined with an ever-growing mountain of debt is problematic to say the least. We all have that person in our life, be it a family member, friend, or mere acquaintance, who is notoriously bad with money. Perhaps you lent them money and found out later that they squandered the money instead of putting it to the purpose they had claimed they'd use it. You soon realize any chance of ever seeing your generosity repaid is slim. The government is like that friend or family member, but unlike that troublesome person who you can ignore or refuse to help, you cannot ignore the federal government. Government will simply send you another vexatious bill in the form of taxation from which you and your family will never benefit.

At some point, the government's largesse will be colossal bill that will require payment. All our collective guest lists are expanding far beyond our inner circles. The same meal we purchased ten years ago now costs significantly more as prices rise, government spending escalates, and increasing inflation seems to be more of a certainty rather than a possibility. At the time of this writing in December of 2021, we are already experiencing inflation rates that we haven't seen in over a decade. Many of my firm's clients are Baby Boomers who will soon transfer significant assets to their children and grandchildren. This will be the single largest transfer of wealth in history. With a national debt loan exceeding $27 trillion today (with $2 trillion added in 2021 alone because of stimulus funding), the government will naturally look to levy heavy taxes on this transfer of wealth to help solve these problems. There is virtually no doubt that our children and their children will shoulder the burden of paying that growing bill if we don't act quickly.

If you are reading this, then chances are high that you are likely among the nation's top 1 percent. You are among an elite group of individuals who have developed (or are developing) a sizable, and in many cases, a *very sizable* estate. You have a lucrative income, have paid an exorbitant amount in taxes, and are rightfully concerned about the direction in which our country is heading. You have also likely felt the burden of picking up the tab too many times. Naturally, you and your family are key resource targets for the government as it attempts to collect revenue in the form of costly taxes to foot the bills that are hanging over our country's figurative head.

The good news is that my firm and I have extensively researched these changing economic and tax circumstances and have outlined the best methods and strategies to ensure you get to dictate which meals you cover and who is on your own personal guest list. I am not sure how long I intend to continue that dinner guest analogy, but I will probably stop using it before the first chapter…probably.

Despite thoroughly researching these changes and creating a system of astute tax-planning strategies, there will undoubtedly still be estate taxes, capital gains taxes, and (of course) income taxes that will come due. However, in this book, I have outlined the contingencies and have formulated the most efficient ways of paying these taxes while simultaneously staying within the confines of the applicable laws. If you are seeking more illicit ways to reduce your taxes, I regret to inform you that you will find none within the pages of this book. However, should you find an advisor who suggests they have such methods up their sleeve and states that you are likely to "get away" with the suggested plans, my advice is to say, "No thank you," and walk quickly away. That advisor probably also has a bridge in Brooklyn to sell you, and I have no doubt they would also suggest the payment for that bridge would be tax deductible!

My track record and that of my associates collectively includes billions of dollars of wealth-transfer programs that have been specifically customized to those which this book is tailored, for 1-percenters like you. You blazed a trail to the top of your business sector by using your intuition and discerning mind, and you took steps to safeguard your finances as well as to ensure your family's generational prosperity. It is with this in mind that I assure you that over the course of four decades, my associates and I have created wealth preservation plans for thousands of our clients who are in that top 1 percent, and who actively seek to:

1. Control who is on their guest list, and who will inherit their wealth.
2. Pay the smallest amount of taxes possible and strategize to pay the taxes that they cannot avoid in the most efficient way possible.
3. Draw tax-free income in retirement wherever feasible.
4. Ensure that the transfer of wealth to future generations is done with the utmost care and attention to detail to avoid unnecessary taxes.

In today's world, instant gratification is easier than ever as technology continues to advance, making our lives easier and our quality of life better. Truly, in today's world of being able to make payments on a plethora of connected devices, obtaining material things is simply a matter of flashing your phone or hitting one key. Technology makes it so easy to spend money on things you'd never have bought if you'd taken some time to consider the outlay. In my family, we still laugh about my aunt who attended her first auction and without meaning to, she ended up the embarrassed owner of a Victorian porcelain chamber pot. She was trying to signal my uncle who had entered the room after circling the neighborhood in search of a parking space. Only a neophyte like my aunt would have used the hand holding the auction paddle to wave to him. In today's world, with one keystroke-you can send money off to a vendor, and the item is yours. Maybe you didn't mean to hit that key, but there may be no way to undo the action. The money is immediately extracted from your account and shot off to the vendor's. This is oh so different from how many of us grew up. In most circumstances back then, people thought it through before committing to an expenditure, even if their reasoning was more of a rationalization and wasn't prudent or based on common sense.

It is easy to be conditioned to chase the highs of business and the market and avoid the tedious yet necessary tasks that need to be completed to secure our futures. Through this book, I will educate you on how to achieve all the above as fully and clearly as possible. I will try to be as humorous as possible, although if my jokes don't land, remember that you are primarily interested in my financial knowledge and strategies, not my remarkably dry sense of humor.

With the backing of hundreds of affluent clients and several nationally recognized accounting firms, our strategies include applicable scenarios and research as well as the experience to affirm why now is the best time for you to plan and prepare for your family's financial future. The design of our proprietary programs helps you retain more wealth, sustain that wealth for your children and grandchildren, and makes sure that you *Don't Pick Up the Bill* for anyone other than those on the guest list you compose.

Who Are We, & Why Should You Trust Us With Your Family's Future?

Throughout this book, I will be using the word *we* often. In my decades of experience in the wealth-planning and creation business, I have learned that no individual can succeed alone not be an expert in all areas of such a diverse and vast industry; it really is a team effort. Like so many others, I grew up playing sports. My experiences in athletics during my formative years prepared me to become a successful coach as an adult, and to this day, I draw upon the lessons that both of those experiences taught me. One of the lessons I learned and experienced season after season was that being a tight-knit team was vital to a team's success. I also discovered that certain traits were imperative to each specific team's success, regardless of how talented any one individual was. Our team includes some of the most devoted and conscientious individuals that I have had the pleasure of working with during my thirty years of experience. Our team consists of some of the top financial, legal, actuarial, and risk- management experts in the industry. We work tirelessly to ensure that every one of our clients benefits from our collective experience and expertise. We are not a large company, but that is not a disadvantage because what our modest roster lacks in quantity, is made up in the quality of our work.

If you cannot tell, I am very proud of my organization. Furthermore, I am honored to be shepherding the direction of an organization founded by my current partner, Joseph W. Tucciarone. When I am asked about him (which is often),

I immediately tell people that in addition to his impressive business prowess and sanguine character, he is also one of the most intelligent people that I know, both inside and outside of our industry. A go-to joke of mine is to tell my clients, "He's very smart. He's a rocket scientist!" Typically, my clients laugh off my remark as a jest, but it's absolutely true! Joe started his career as an aerospace engineer and worked to help put the first men on the moon as part of the Apollo program. (If you're ever on a game show, he's the perfect choice for a phone-a-friend lifeline call!) Now I am sure many companies in this industry will boast about their professionals being the cream of the crop and the brightest and most skilful in their field, but how many of them can say that one of their colleagues literally helped to put the first man on the moon?

For more than thirty years, our team has provided sophisticated financial solutions and extraordinary personal service to our clients, accounting firms, and advisory professionals. Since the founding of our organization, the goal has always been to provide an unparalleled level of education, support, and personal service to our clients. This goal has been integral in building the ongoing relationships with our clients who are the very foundation of our firm. We respect our clients and their goals for their futures and those of their heirs. We never suggest a cookie-cutter financial plan; our job is to listen to the client, scour the available options, and devise a plan that utilizes financial instruments that are uniquely suited to the client's situation and financial status. Our company feels that much like a family business, and despite our growth and client roster, we have retained the familiarity and ease with which we collaborate and work with one another to better serve our clients. This signature attribute is quite frankly unparalleled in our industry.

One of the things we take pride in is the lengths to which we are willing to go to inform and educate our clients about the state of the financial world, the various financial instruments that are attractive today, and especially about the financial strategies we propose for them. That desire to educate and inform is the impetus behind this book, which I'm certain you won't be able to bear to put down as it will quickly become your favorite book on wealth planning. Of course, I know the competition is stiff, but hey, don't forget that my partner is a rocket scientist.

In addition to numbers of satisfied clients that can provide testament to our firm's exemplary work, we also specialize in working as a team with our clients' *other* advisors, especially their accountants. Because of this, we have fostered strong relationships with some of the world's top financial institutions. We do this to guarantee that our clients will receive a first-rate service that will be unrivalled by anyone else in our field, but it's also to broaden our horizons by networking and learning from the leading innovators in every associated field. The ultimate objective of this book is to educate you on how to protect your assets for generations to come. It is not an exaggeration to suggest that applying the strategies laid out within these pages over your lifetime could result in tens of millions of dollars being kept in your pocket instead of going into Uncle Sam's. An added plus is that this can all be accomplished with no discernible impact on your current finances. It's all in a day's work for us.

Chapter 1

Congratulations! Sort of...

Throughout history, there have been cataclysmic events that not only affected life at the time, but also continued to affect the lives of subsequent generations. Regardless of how predictable or unforeseen these events were, people's liveli- hoods were subject to what can be thought of as a stress test. As a result, some fortunes blossomed while others crumbled into obscurity. While some circumstances such as the COV- ID-19 Pandemic or the 9/11 terrorist attack on the World Trade Center could not have been predicted nor thus adequately pre- pared for, others can be foreseen, and appropriate planning can and should be put in place to mitigate any repercussions.

Since you chose to read this book, I am confident that the chances are good that you are an affluent individual concerned with the future of your wealth and assets; you yearn for the best way to ensure they are inherited by your progeny as smoothly as conceivable, and with as little as possible going to taxes. Alternatively, you might be one of our clients who just cannot get enough of listening to me talk about wealth planning, and you intend for my written words to keep you company on a lonely night. Whatever your reason may be, I can assure you that if there was not an exigent reason to do so, I would not be allocating a significant portion of my time to writing an entire book on the subject. And what is this subject exactly? Taxes — income taxes, capital gains taxes, estate taxes. Let me say it another way — taxes.

Taxes are a constant in life. As many of you can attest, taxes have also been an incessant talking point for administrations on both sides of the aisle since the Thirteenth Amendment was ratified in 1913 and gave Congress the right to levy a federal income tax. Federal taxes have been a sore subject since President Lincoln's move to tax income in 1862.

You may be thinking that if politicians have always blustered about taxes and what they intend to do regarding them, what makes the present day's politicians' plans any more ominous than those cooked up in the past?

The answer is that asset transfer I mentioned earlier. Older Americans, primarily the generation known as the Baby Boomers, have spent the past few decades procuring a truly staggering amount of money. Their wealth, which is equal to a whopping 157 percent of America's gross domestic product, has begun to be dispersed to their heirs and other beneficiaries. As of the end of 2021, Americans aged seventy and above had a collective net worth of nearly $35 trillion. Even to the wealthiest among us, that is a truly staggering amount. It's a number so vast that it is difficult to conceptualize. While the process of handing this wealth down to future generations has already begun, it is estimated that by 2042, as much as $70 trillion will have been handed down from Baby Boomers to their heirs. This older generation of Americans is beginning to flex their economic muscles, and many are not waiting until death or retirement to begin dispersing their wealth. From 2010 to 2016, the IRS reported that the collective amount of annual gifts increased from $45 billion to $75 billion. It is noteworthy to mention that this data only reflects what has been reported, and the bulk of what has been gifted flies under the radar of the IRS. That makes sense because the total amount of tax-exempt gifts allowed has risen dramatically in the past ten years; in 2010, it was $1 million for individuals and $2 million for couples, and today it stands at $11.7 million for individuals and $23.4 million for couples.

If you are stunned by those numbers, rest assured that you are not the only one to have taken notice. The Biden Administration's American Families Plan potentially threatened to nearly double current capital gains taxes, effectively hamstringing the process of estate planning that wealthy Americans have reliably used for generations. If it had been taken into effect, the plan would have raised the top capital gains rate from 23.8 percent to a whopping 43.4 percent, and the plan could have even started to tax assets upon death as if they'd been sold. For those who own assets such as stocks or real estate, or who have businesses that have boomed exponentially over the years, this may become worrisome, especially when the time comes to pass wealth along to beneficiaries.

While at the time of this writing it seems that the plan will not be passed, the proposals on the table have been a frightening-forewarning to the top 1 percent. Current tax levels that were adopted in the Tax Cuts and Jobs Act of 2017 are set to end in 2025; tax rates will then rise significantly on affluent Americans, their businesses, and their estates, even if no other increases are passed before that time. The tax proposals of 2021 should serve as a wake-up call and cautionary tale. As we have witnessed this past year, it's time to make sure your assets and plans are arranged in the most efficient before things change. When did Noah build the ark? Before it started raining.

However, the Biden Administration's American Families Plan is not the sole threat to wealth held by the 1 percent. It is likely to be enacted in conjunction with other proposed legislation that is intended to balance the federal budget by increasing taxes on the 1 percent.

Why Should You be Concerned?

Proposed changes to estate taxation planning have uncovered distressing financial vulnerabilities that have resulted in a surge among our clients to request a review of their estate plans. As you know, taxes tend to be fickle; I'm certain we can all agree on that. Regardless of whether you have already heard of the upcoming transfer of wealth, or if this book is serving as the harbinger of the change yet to come, pre-emptive action is of paramount importance in preventing taxes from gobbling up a substantial chunk of your wealth.

Current legislative trends pose a significant threat to corporations and high-net-worth individuals. A $1 trillion bipartisan infrastructure bill was passed by the Senate on August 1, 2021, by a vote of 69-30. It was designed to pour $550 billion into America's crumbling infrastructure to include bridges, roads, airports, and infrastructure to service electric vehicles.

The Biden Administration has proposed many ways to finance the costs associated with the bill including taxes on corporations and high-net-worth individuals. The administration has also called for increasing the personal income tax to 39.6 percent on persons earning $400,000 or more per year. Additionally, it would increase payroll taxes on incomes above $400,000 as a means of funding Social Security.

In March 2021, wealthy individuals were targeted by legislators other than the Biden Administration through proposed bills including the Ultra-Millionaire Tax Act, the the 99.5 Percent Act, and the Sensible Taxation and Equity Promotion (STEP) Act. On March 1, 2021, Senator Elizabeth Warren introduced The Ultra-Millionaire Tax Act, which would impose an annual tax of 2 percent on the net wealth of households and trusts valued at +$50 million - $1 billion, with an added annual surtax of 1 percent on households and trusts valued at over $1 billion.

A few weeks later, on March 25, 2021, Warren was followed by Senator Bernie Sanders' proposal, For the 99.5 Percent Act, which is the most comprehensive overhaul of estate planning of all the proposed bills. The proposal included the following changes in estate planning: (i) lowering the amounts for estate tax exemption to $3.5 million and the gift tax exemption to $1 million; (ii) a graduated raise in estate tax rates ranging from 45 percent up to 65 percent; (iii) elimination of specific discounts for family-owned entities; (iv) requiring Grantor Retained Annuity Trusts (GRATs) to have a 10-year minimum term and a minimum remainder interest of the greater of $500,000 or 25 percent of the amount contributed; ending GST tax-exempt trusts after fifty years; and (vi) tightening the annual gift tax exclusion, which is presently $15,000 per individual, to limiting each donor to a cumulative $30,000 annual gift tax exclusion regardless of the number of individuals for certain transfers.

In addition, the For the 99.5 Percent Act would have required significant changes in estate grantor trusts by calling for: (i) assets in a grantor trust will be included in the grantor's estate; (ii) treating distributions from a grantor trust as gifts from the grantor, and (iii) treating the entire trust as a gift from the grantor if grantor trust status is "turned off" during the life of the grantor.

Then on March 29, 2021, shortly after Sanders' bill was introduced, Senator Chris Van Hollen introduced The STEP Act. The STEP Act takes aim at basis step-up by taxing property transferred by gift in trust or upon death as if it were being sold for its fair market value; this would impose capital gains taxes immediately. The exemption for any such gain would be limited to $1 million. Finally, all "non-grantor" trusts would be taxed on unrealized gains every twenty-one years.

Even if Congress and the Senate do not pass these proposed bills into law, existing exemptions for estate taxes including federal estate, gift, and GST tax are all scheduled to expire by 2025. If they are allowed to expire, the exemptions would be automatically reduced by approximately 50 percent, returning to their former basis of $5 million per individual, indexed for inflation. While certain exclusions may be retained, such as $1 million per person plus $250,000 for a personal residence, it is advisable to consider the implications for capital gains prior to 2025. Although there are concerns at present about high inflation, the indexed exemption for 2026 is projected to be approximately $6.4 million per individual.

While the Biden Administration's proposals for the 2022

budget and the tax reforms proposed by Sanders, Warren, and Van Hollen are unlikely to be enacted in their original forms, the proposals should still serve as a warning to high-net-worth individuals to review their existing estate plans and to actively search for ways to protect their estates in the near term before legislation is passed that will adversely affect them.

No matter how smart we are, even if we acquire more rocket scientists like Joe to work with us, we cannot predict the future with any kind of certainty. However, we do have historical data and trends that we can study and analyze. Yet while these can certainly be good indicators, they also cannot assure guarantees. I will do my best to avoid speaking in absolutes. However, I firmly believe taxes will go up regardless of whether these newly proposed tax rates are exact or not. The government has a proclivity toward increasing taxes on the wealthy to fund the ever-growing budget deficit. There is a cycle of ballooning expenses, raised taxes, and so on, forcing this cycle on an upswing. Like nearly everything that involves the federal government, this will undoubtedly take time to take effect. If your strategy is to put off preparing for the worst in the hopes that a new administration will come along in a few years and scale back taxes, beware! I would strongly advise against it. Sure, a new administration may certainly propose lower taxes on the wealthy, but that does not mean they won't eventually set their sights on *your* money. To reiterate an earlier point, this is the largest wealth transfer in history, with an estimate of $70 trillion forecasted to exchange hands by 2042. Don't think you've got plenty of time to get ready. Twenty years may sound like all the time in the world to you now, but those years will pass in the blink of an eye. No one wants to be scrambling around, trying in vain to protect assets that Uncle Sam has his eye on, only to be told by every financial advisor they consult that it is just too late; there isn't enough time to put the plans in place and avoid full taxation.

Regardless of what political party controls Congress or

the White House, no one in the government is foolish enough to let those funds transfer hands without using taxation to get a sizable chunk for the government's use. And could you blame them? They are simply doing what any sane, logical, and practical person would do in that position. And this is coming from someone who does not think very highly of the government's acquisition and subsequent spending of taxes (if you could not tell from my subtle and sheepish rhetoric regarding them in the introduction of this book). But rather than dressing up like a Mohawk Indian and tossing tea into Boston Harbor in errant protest, I am trying to be constructive by educating the masses in an act of docile protest. The pen is mightier than the sword, after all.

If you are alarmed, concerned, or anxious, don't worry; those are perfectly normal reactions. However, before you become too disillusioned with the future of your wealth, allow me to take a machete to your financial thicket. There are a plethora of options built into the tax code that I can help you take full advantage of, and I intend to. Trusts, tax-free accumulation products, and captive insurance are just a few of these options that I will cover extensively in this book. Some of these may work splendidly for you, while others may not. My firm and I have devoted considerable time to studying these changes and outlining contingencies, and we have devised the most efficacious strategies to adroitly navigate the shifting tax paradigm. Regardless of what works for you and what does not, stagnation is unacceptable and could have devastating repercussions for the estate you have worked hard to establish. You cannot sit back and hope your wealth and assets will increase and be available for you to enjoy and then pass on to your heirs. In the words of the great Vince Lombardi, "Hope is not a strategy." He was right. It's fine to have hopes and dreams for your future, but you've got to put a foundation under that castle in the sky. The foundation is your solid plan to achieve those hopes and dreams. You must take the time to work with your advisor to develop a strategy for wealth preservation and growth, and *you must stick to it.* Preparing for the future takes a plan, determination, and discipline.

While economic activity may flourish under one elected official and wither under another, remember that the most significant wealth transfer in history looms on the horizon, and no matter who is at the helm in the coming years, that person is going to want a piece of that delectable pie. The transmission of wealth from the Baby Boomers to their heirs is becoming my constant refrain, I know. Please don't fail to heed my repeated warnings. There will undoubtedly be significant changes to the tax code so the federal government can snare as much of that wealth as possible. Whether you are a Baby Boomer about to pass along your fortune to your heirs or you are a Baby Boomer's heir, you need to pay close attention to what Congress does and learn how to mitigate your bill.

Within the confines of this book, I will lay out the roadmap to handling these impending changes. Whether you are green in this department with little to no plan, or you are an economic savant, there is something to be learned from this book. Be patient, bear with me, and upon finishing this book, I am more than confident that you will be steadfastly serene in the face of any new changes or developments.

My ultimate goal is to get you and your heirs to a place where the changes in the tax code (as they apply to wealth transfer) make little to no difference to get you to a place where you stop worrying about what party is in office or what the next administration may do. Our plans are predominantly focused on making sure that enough of your legacy assets are arranged outside of your estate in tax-advantaged vehicles, while still giving you the control that I know is deeply important to the vast majority of you.

There is so much more to come that will showcase the research my team and I have done, and to finally put the strategies we have studied and carefully formulated into print. Absolutely none of this would ever have been possible without all the long hours that my colleagues put in creating wealth management and estate plans for our clients. None of this would it be possible without the trust that my clients have in my ability to provide them with these services. Later in the book, I'll explain the difference between a suitability standard of care and a fiduciary standard of care. I absolutely and always adhere to a fiduciary standard of care when I work with my clients. They are vibrant individuals who have achieved great things in their chosen endeavours and fields. I am grateful and blessed for the opportunity to know and assist each and every one of them.

You and I may never meet in person, but don't let that stop you from using the tips and information I'm sharing in this book to improve your financial status. Let's get started on the path to save some money by reducing your current and future tax bill.

Chapter 2

Life Insurance: A Misunderstood Sector

Before you roll your eyes and pre-judge this strategy, please bear with me because this is an imperative element of estate planning, regardless of the stereotypical images that may be flooding your thoughts.

> ***There is a strategy that creates, preserves, and grows wealth with such efficiency that not only is the wealth transferred without being subject to estate tax, but it also continues to grow income tax free, while simultaneously allowing you to withdraw income in the later years on a very favorable and unique tax basis.***

You may think this sounds too good to be true and may question why you have not heard of it before. Well, you have probably heard it in some fashion, but because it involves the words *life insurance,* you no doubt discounted it. For many people, life insurance conjures up bad memories of inept salesmen, high commissions, and low return on investment. As I mentioned earlier, I have worked in the financial industry for more than three decades, and while I can say with all sincerity that this industry attracts some of the brightest of human minds, it also attracts some of the dimmest people. The true professionals in our business serve their clients well and do important work protecting families, businesses, and wealth. However, there is also no shortage of troglodytes in the industry who have no discernible attributes suited for finance other than being *just good enough* at selling in order to get by, although in some cases, they somehow are able to line their own pockets quite well. For the most part, those charlatans are easy to spot, especially if you are halfway knowledgeable about financial concepts. Regardless, many salesmen of that ilk flock to the life insurance sector where they push financial instruments with a focus on their commission rather than on what suits the client. Because of their ineptitude and greed, the reputation of life insurance agents has been tarnished. Now, let's be realistic; every business and every industry has its bad actors. It just seems that life insurance salesmen have been the brunt of jokes for as long as I can remember, and the truth is, these jokes are not far off the mark.

Over my career, I have had the great privilege to work with and learn from some of the most intelligent, creative, and well-respected professionals in our business. And, yes, some of them have handled life insurance for their clients. They taught me well how to identify and implement the very best wealth planning, creation, and preservation strategies, especially as applied to utilizing life insurance for affluent and ultra-affluent clients.

The core strategies that we implement utilizing life insurance are structured and designed in a way that you probably have not seen before.

Though you almost certainly may not have thought of using life insurance in such a way yourself, the concept may sound familiar to you. That is because it is structured in the very same way that large banks and corporations buy and invest in life insurance on what we like to refer to as an *institutionally* or *commercially priced* basis. Perhaps the most glaring problem in how life insurance is bought and sold within the retail market is the excessive expenses built into the product. If you guessed that commissions are one of the main culprits, then you are spot on. For example, commissions on certain whole or other permanent life policies can range from

70 percent to 120 percent of the first year's premium. While the higher commission load on these policies undoubtedly makes agents within the sector very happy, it also creates a significant drag on the financial efficiency of the product. In effect, this renders use of this technique for a wealth planning strategy problematic to say the least, and it gives it the lousy reputation known to so many people.

> ***My goal is to completely change this paradigm and show our affluent clientele how to buy and use this financial instrument in a way that mimics what larger institutions use, thereby creating something exciting and practical in the process.***

But let's get real; we are not completely altruistic in our approach. While our structure allows us to provide our clients with tens of millions of dollars' worth of life insurance to be utilized in this strategy efficiently, and even at a much lower compensation level per million, we are still compensated quite well. And this is something that should only be done within this context; you typically would not buy this amount of life insurance if the policies were placed on a retail basis.

After reading the next two chapters, you will have a good understanding of our strategies and how to implement them most effectively. Both Chapters 3 and 4 are critical — likely the most significant in the book. There are many facets of life — like health and family — that are monumentally more important than money. With rare exception, most people would agree with that statement; I think people would go to great lengths to provide for and protect their loved ones.

Most readers of this book are looking for ways to protect their wealth from the rapacious hands of the government. The driving force behind such action is the continued comfort and protection this wealth brings to their family. While family, security, and peace of mind are preeminent to most (if not all) aspects of life, that is not to say money is not a major player in life. Your financial status directly and indirectly influences many of the previously mentioned aspects. The best times in your life are enhanced when your finances are flourishing; the lows and woes of your life are exacerbated if your financial status is dire. Nonetheless, we have established that there are more important things in life than a little bit of money...and one of them is a *whole lot* of money.

The following chapters will outline strategies for protecting your wealth and will serve as the vehicle to provide the financial security and freedom coveted by so many. Both Chapters 3 and 4 will cover these strategies. But for clarity, I have strategically split them into two chapters because depending upon the strategy being discussed, it may be more appropriate to use either at different stages of your life. It must be noted that while we will discuss a variety of strategies, no one system is superior to all others, and each serves its intended purpose. What works best for you will be determined by a multitude of factors that are likely to change throughout your life. Use both Chapters 3 and 4 to guide you in the right direction.

Chapter 3

The Strategy for the Established Affluent (Ages 40-60)

The first strategy I will discuss in this chapter is something we like to call *Option Life 2™*. (This is what others in our industry refer to in the general category of *premium financing*.) This strategy allows you to acquire very large amounts of life insurance with very little out-of-pocket cost. (Translation: Ron will show you a way *not* to have to pay premiums on lots of tax-favored life insurance, especially since most life insurance premiums are paid with after-tax dollars.) While it is certainly a dynamic strategy, Option Life 2™ is directed toward our younger clientele. The reason it is more appropriate for those clients between the ages of forty to sixty (in general) is that for the transaction to operate most safely, there needs to be a timeframe that is typically greater than twenty-five years.

This strategy addresses three major goals:

1. To protect our families and businesses in a very tax and cashflow-efficient manner.
2. To grow a significant asset that can be used to generate tax-free income in retirement.
3. To most efficiently pay estate taxes if and when they become due.

While our younger clients may not be too focused on estate taxes currently, it's something that needs to be considered as part of their overall planning. The asset we create here assumes the form of a large, tax-free benefit paid out to the client's beneficiaries. This method also helps pay estate taxes. That way, even if Washington DC imposes high estate taxes, we can offset them using Option Life 2™. If estate taxes are low, your heirs will get additional tax-free wealth. If set up correctly, premium financing for younger affluent clientele can also set up what will eventually become a nice income stream later in life — millions of dollars that could never be acquired from a conventional pension or 401(k) instrument.

The Option Life 2™ transaction is structured in such a way as to create an asset for not only the client's heirs, but also for the client. Additionally, a good portion of the life insurance policy expenses, such as commissions, are removed from the equation altogether. If this concept sounds familiar, you may be aware that ***this is the way institutions such as banks and large corporations buy life insurance and utilize the product. By having our affluent clients following suit, what is created is essentially an institutionally priced policy that subsequently turns the typical life insurance approach from an expense into an asset.*** The aforementioned asset comes in the form of a large benefit paid out to an individual's beneficiaries and is tax free, of course. In addition to creating a significantly more tax-efficient avenue for wealth transfer, this method also helps pay estate taxes. This allows our clients and their heirs the freedom to have peace of mind about Washington D.C. and the government's whimsical tax law changes. If estate taxes are high, you are prepared; if they are low, your heirs will get additional tax-free wealth. Our clients sleep well at night knowing that their plan is bulletproof from a tax point of view. If set up correctly, premium financing for younger affluent clientele can also set up what will eventually become a nice income stream later in life. We are talking about millions and millions of dollars here, the kind of money that could never be acquired from a pension or 401(k) plan because of the limitations put on the annual contributions. We can genuinely turn life insurance from an expense into a significant asset on your personal financial balance sheet and that of your heirs.

Not surprisingly, many affluent and high-net-worth individuals are approached with life insurance premium financing proposals. These proposals are always enticing because they appear to offer *free insurance.* But like most things in life, there is some cost attached, even if it is well hidden. You must be very, *very* careful in those cases. If these policies are structured or funded incorrectly, if the expense drag on the policies is too high, or if the policies are not monitored every single year, you could have major problems on your hands down the road. One of the main reasons that accounting firms work with our company is because of our diligent follow-up and attention to detail. We try to make the Option Life 2™ process, or premium financing as it is known by many, as straightforward as possible.

The strategy is simple: A lender makes a loan to a policyowner. In most cases this will be an irrevocable life insurance trust (ILIT). It is done this way to ensure that premiums are paid on the policy which is owned by the trust. This can be accomplished exclusively because in our structure, we have created a true asset that can be loaned against almost any other asset with equity value. To reiterate, the policy is priced on an institutional basis rather than a retail basis and becomes an asset, not an expense. Now, assuming the loans continue for the entirety of the policy's premium-paying term at the projected interest rate, and the policy performs as illustrated (based upon a very conservative look at decades of historical performance), then the policy's cash value should be more than sufficient at a specified point in the transaction to reap the bank loan and interest accrued. The death benefit would ultimately be paid to the ILIT income tax free and be transferred to the insured's heir's estate, tax free.

In order for this transaction to be compliant with regulatory and insurance company regulations, the client must have some financial investment or *skin in the game.* In this transaction, the client's skin in the game comes from the necessity to post what I will call *gap collateral* for the loan. You need to exercise great caution if anyone pitches you *free insurance* where there is no exposure whatsoever. As we discussed earlier, that individual is in the same league as the infamous guy "selling you the Brooklyn bridge." Since the asset is the insurance policy itself, we can use that asset to collateralize the bulk of the loan.

Our chart below shows that the policy has significant equity value because of its institutional pricing and methodology of funding, even in year one. The difference between that equity value and the total loan is the gap. The client must post that gap collateral to secure the loan. The collateral can be posted in bank accounts, brokerage accounts, the cash value of other life insurance policies, or just about any liquid asset that is available. The necessity for collateral will increase for a period of time as the loan grows. There will then come a crossover point at which time the policy's equity value surpasses the total loan due. At that time, current collateral will be released and there should be no need for additional collateral; the asset will be collateralizing itself.

Male Age 45

$50,000,000 Initial Death Benefit

Policy Rate of Return Normal Assumption - $5.5%
Loan Interest Rate Normal Assumption - 2% Rising to 4.5%

	Annual Financing	Total Loan*	Policy Cash Value	Projected Collateral Needed (Normal)**	Projected Collateral Needed 25% Stress***	Death Benefit After Loan
1	$3,170,526	$3,234,817	$1,765,034	$1,558,035	$1,725,713	$49,634,067
5	$3,170,526	17,239,372	15,597,338	2,421,901	3,459,124	49,036,566
10	$3,170,526	38,300,525	37,934,983	2,262,291	4,635,743	49,751,008
15	$3,170,526	44,587,832	48,056,486	0	2,129,127	45,058,654
20	$3,170,526	57,923,304	68,529,861	0	0	45,074,235
30	$3,170,526	0	28,131,285	0	0	55,410,000
40	$3,170,526	0	60,781,570	0	0	84,327,237

**Loan repaid from policy in Year 21*

*** Under normal assumptions collateral will be released in year 11 as the policy cash value exceeds the total loan*

**** This assumes that projections of policy returns and borrowing rates are 25% higher that original assumptions*

Disclaimer: This is an explanation of a typical premium finance transaction. It is not intended to represent any specific carrier or any specific client. It is not a solicitation to buy insurance and should be used for informational purposes only. Hypothetical values and rates are *for demonstrative purposes only and do not represent any investments available in the market*

The chart illustrates how this strategy can be realistically used if it is appropriately executed. While lending assets to pay insurance premiums, a lending institution will establish a lien against the policy for a specified number of years. To maximize growth and eventually repay the loan from the policy itself, policy values are invested in accounts that mirror specific stock indices. The initial loan is set up in such a way as to cover the premiums, and in most cases, the interest and any other fees required to secure the loan. At the top of the illustration, you can see that a rising LIBOR interest rate is projected for illustrative purposes, and assumptions of rate of return are made for the index accounts that hold the insurance policy's assets. Both the bank interest rates and policy rates of return will vary, and the outside collateral requirements needed to be provided by the insured will be determined based upon the type of collateral that is pledged. Bank interest rate increases or policy performance that is less than expected could result in the client having to pay some of the interest on the loan out of pocket. Or what is more likely, the collateral necessary to be posted could be on the higher end of the illustrative projections.

All these possibilities are given close scrutiny and, considered from every angle when we conduct a stringent *stress test* of our illustrations and projections as we build a customized plan for each client. The key to taking the risk out of this type of structure is time. If there is enough time on the client's side (think twenty years or more), the lending and equity markets can go through their typical and cyclical ups and downs. This allows us to become very comfortable with the reliability of our stress testing while providing our clients with a transaction that gives them the absolute best possibility of achieving all the goals we set.

Speaking of equity markets, in most cases the policies we use to fund these financing transactions are known as Indexed Universal Life Insurance (IUL). The premiums and cash values are invested in a unique combination of the insurance company's general account to provide downside protection -and- index options to provide upside growth similar to returns on the S&P 500 (or other select indices). The key here is to reduce market volatility and allow the policy to grow at a reasonable rate of return. (Think 5 percent to 5.5 percent.) While the S&P 500 is a stable index and fairly predictable over long periods of time, we must reduce volatility further by using an option strategy. The key feature of this policy class is that while they track market index performance for the investment of their cash values, they are hedged so that the rate of return can never drop below 0 percent in any given year. Assuming there was $1 million in cash value and the stock market dropped 50 percent in a crash, the investment account on such a policy would remain flat.

"That sounds too good to be true, Ron. There must be a catch." That is what I hear most often when I describe an IUL policy. There is no catch per se, but there is a trade-off. While the floor is protected, there is also a cap on the upside of the market performance of generally 8.5 to 11 percent depending on the specific policy. So, in a year during which the S&P 500 is up 25 percent, the policy would only be credited with the cap rate. As you can see, we have taken out the highs and the lows and focused on stable, more dependable returns in our long-term portfolio.

Our client's collateral requirements are initially projected to be $1.5M in year one, but they will rise to a peak of $2.2M over the life of their loan. Our client's collateral requirements may increase in the event the policy's performance does not meet historical expectations over a long period of time or if an adverse long-term trend in loan interest rates occurs. Remember, the objective is to use the policy cash-surrender value to pay back the loan while leaving the policy intact.

Once we have paid back the loan, we can then start focusing on drawing tax-free income from the policy. Assuming our assumptions were good, we monitored policy and loan performance each year, and made any necessary adjustments to the transaction, in most cases there is the opportunity to draw millions of dollars in tax-free income from the policy while leaving a healthy death benefit for our heirs.

In our illustration, the death benefit that would be paid out to the beneficiaries would start at $49.6M, and at the age of eight-five is projected to be $80 million. However, the client could have also elected to take tax-free millions of dollars income during their lifetime and a lower ultimate death benefit. This illustrates the tremendous amount of flexibility and tax efficiency built into this program. Remember, this is a hypothetical example of how a policy can perform and an actual policy can result in higher or lower death benefits, and cash values.

In review, what have we accomplished here using our leveraged Option Life 2™ strategy? Take a look:

- We have acquired tens of millions of dollars of tax-free death benefits for our families, our businesses, and eventually for our heirs.
- We have accomplished this while paying no after-tax premium.
- We have created the opportunity for millions of dollars of tax-free income in retirement.
- All that, and what has it cost? Our out-of-pocket cost could be minimal to nothing.

It's not free, but what in life is?

You must have the ability and assets to post the necessary collateral depending upon the performance of the plan, and then have the balance sheet necessary to qualify for the loan.

This type of transaction may seem familiar. This is how our clients buy real estate, businesses, and other significant assets. They use leverage, they use other people's money, they understand and control their risks, and they have the vision and foresight to see the power in these types of asset acquisitions. What they don't generally do is pay cash with after-tax dollars, although most of my industry asks clients to do so in situations where there are significantly more efficient options.

For example, let's say that someone wants to pay the premium for such a policy all on their own. The death benefit would still be a substantially positive investment for their heirs. By looking at the internal rate of return (IRR) on the death benefit (relative to premiums paid) considering the client's life expectancy, there is still a cash-on-cash rate of return between 6 to 7 percent which is tax free. Considering this can be viewed and categorized as a fixed asset class, this rate of return is still far above what the individual could expect from other fixed type investments for legacy asset investments. For instance, if someone could guarantee you 6 to 7 percent tax- free income on municipal bonds and lock that in for thirty years, would you make that investment for your children or grandchildren? You'd be silly not to take them up on it because there is nowhere on Wall Street where you could get anywhere close to such a deal. The only risk posed to the client is if they outlived their predicted life expectancy. Should this occur, then the rate of return would obviously decrease. It's important to note that the client cannot ever lose money; their rate of return will always be positive. And, in the event of a longer than expected lifespan, they would consequently enjoy many additional years among family and loved ones.

Regardless of how attractive a proposal such as this looks, the viability and allure of premium financing is dependent upon a multitude of underlying assumptions. These include the amount and renewability of premium-financing loans, interest payments or accruals, the interest rate charged on the loan, collateral, loan repayment, and of course, the actual performance of the policy in question. Your advisor needs to know the assumptions and be knowledgeable of all aspects of the policy and your financial situation. That should go without saying (especially if you are working with one of our NNA advisors), but it is an essential point in determining that the investment is right for you. As we have done numerous times in the past, we structure this policy so that the bulk of commissions and fees, which are typically associated with the life insurance portion of the policy including the lion's share of the cost to the policyholder, are significantly reduced.

You may be asking yourself why we would lessen the otherwise lucrative fees and commissions that would go into our own pockets. That is a perfectly understandable question, especially given the history of life insurance with its plethora of fees and commissions. The answer is simple; we are more than confident that this is an excellent option for many of our affluent clients, particularly those on the younger side. While we undoubtedly will miss out on higher commissions, we revel in the chance to take this opportunity to shamelessly brag that we would instead choose a strategy and subsequent policy that is in the best interest of our clients rather than focusing on lining our own pockets. You do not get to be in business for as many decades as we have (humble brag) by taking the greedy route.

For younger clientele, who I like to call the established affluent, premium financing can mitigate the premium payments and create a leveraged asset transaction. Assuming everything goes as planned, we can also add significant tax-free income to retirement years using a good form of leverage. Most of the collateral for such a financing structure would be provided by the policy; the client would be required to only post additional collateral. In unlikely scenarios, our diligent monitoring of the transaction potentially could pay some interest on the loan at some point in the future. Even if that were to occur, we would be able to demonstrate that the transaction was still a huge financial win for our client and their heirs. Of course, these financial structures would have to endure our stringent stress tests, and the client would have to be aware of the potential downside risk to the transaction.

Although these transactions are structured with the utmost care and can be quite beneficial, there is usually a downside to everything, and that needs to be taken into consideration.

Now for my older, established, and more venerable clients, premium financing is generally not recommended because of the restricted timeframe of the transaction based upon the client's age. For those clients, we will look toward the strategies I will discuss in Chapter 4.

Ultimately, we favor this strategy because its techniques do not rely upon laws and regulations that Congress is likely to change any time soon, and it would not be challenged by the IRS.

It is highly improbable that the nature of utilizing an irrevocable trust or the tax benefits corresponding to life insurance in general are going to come under attack or be changed. Now that is not to say that changes do not happen, and that we would not respond appropriately by utilizing advanced planning techniques based upon a client's individual needs, goals, and desires. However, our strategy should be the bedrock of the plan since it addresses the three most common issues most of our clients face: cost, income, and control.

CHAPTER 4

The Strategy for the Mature Affluent (Ages 60-80)

For affluent clientele that are even more established, a bit more shall we say … *mature* … the earlier strategy of premium financing is not generally recommended. Although there are situations from time to time in which we can use certain finance techniques, it really depends on our client's age, situation, and frankly, their risk tolerance. The limitations are primarily due to the shortened timeframe (think life expectancy) available for the transaction based upon the client's age. While financing strategies are not ideal for someone older, that does not mean there are no other tactics better suited for the mature affluent client.

A stark difference between the established affluent clients we talked about in Chapter 3 and their more venerable counterparts in this chapter is how they look at their assets when passing them to their heirs. As with many aspects of life, our younger clients have time on their side. They are afforded the luxury of planting seeds that will not be sown for many years to come, allowing their heirs to reap the benefits. The mature affluent simply do not have the time that would be necessary for these strategies to yield their fruits and therefore would not be worth implementing. Luckily, several more viable options are available unless you prefer writing hefty checks to Uncle Sam.

Your Wealth Tower & Efficient Generational Planning

Efficiency is, well, efficient. Regardless of the context, whether it be keeping up with workflow at the office or managing the upkeep of your home, most would agree that striving for efficiency is a lifelong practice that is beneficial in just about every aspect of our lives. The Japanese word for efficiency is *Kanban.* That word rolls off the tongue so much more smoothly than its English counterpart. When I consider the extraordinary number of people who do not speak Japanese but have chosen a Japanese word for a tattoo, I think *Kanban* would be a better choice than the typical *water* or *peace* that most have branded on themselves. (Or that's what they think the ink says. I'm sure we've all read about people who have asked for a Japanese word like *peace* to be tattooed on a limb only to discover later that it's a meaningless mark or a rude word instead.) Although we are the first in the estate planning world to utilize this word, we are hardly the first entity to associate the term with our products. In the past, both Toyota and Bill Gates have used this Japanese word for structuring and designing their products and processes slated for long-term planning.

When discussing this plan, we use an example to help our clients visualize how a Kanban approach to estate planning can be both efficient in avoiding unnecessary outlays for taxes and in safeguarding their estate for their heirs while giving them peace of mind. First, we ask our clients to draw a basic picture of a large office building tower. After coming to terms with our unorthodox approach to educating them, most people draw something that ends up looking like this:

Some are much more creative than others, but this is the typical picture. Next, we explain to the client that this tower represents their net wealth stacked from dollar one to their current total net worth. So, we add something representative of their wealth:

Regardless of the actual figure of their net worth and whether it is higher or lower than that listed in the chart, the application of the exercise will not be affected in any way. Next, we ask our clients what the bottom of the barrel would be, the absolute lowest, imaginable number their total net worth couldn't ever realistically drop below — their worst-case scenario. (The stock market tanks, business is alarmingly horrible, a pandemic locks everyone in their homes for a year … you get the idea.) Usually, the first answer is something coy (in the example above, they might say $29.5 million) so we prod them a little more. After getting them to go lower and lower, and then maybe just a bit lower, we state very pointedly, "Give us an amount that you would sooner jump off that building you just drew if your net worth dropped below. What number would that be?"

This usually shakes the shyness out of them. We often still need to nudge the numbers down with them, and typically the lowest amount they ever go down to is roughly 25 percent of their current total wealth. For this example, it would look something like this:

As you can imagine, no one is comfortable with the final number, regardless of what it is. But the exercise is not finished yet. Now we look back at their total net worth graph and ask them a question that takes them by surprise… "how much of that money is yours"?

After getting the typical, somewhat perplexed look, I hear, "Of course, all of it is mine, Ron." That is the characteristic response I get to this question, even thoughthat is not necessarily the case. As previously stated, and despite what that bottom of the barrel amount might be, it must be understood that they just told us they would never be touching those funds. The specific context in which we ask the question should prompt our client to state the amount that would make them jump off the building they just drew. So, even if it *is*

technically their money, it's money they never intended to spend; they would go over the edge if their net worth sunk that low. Although they would likely never spend that money, that is not to say that it had no value to them; that money would probably go straight to their heirs. The money currently sitting at the bottom of your wealth pool, while stagnant, is still an integral facet of your dynastic wealth.

The continued protection of this successional wealth so that it may one day be transferred to the next generation is the foundation for estate planning; it's the method by which your family will continue to thrive for future generations. So, while you (hopefully) will never need to dip into that bottom of the barrel figure, do not think it does not serve a crucial purpose. To reinforce this foundation, you must make sound financial decisions that strengthen the value of your investments and income, both directly and passively. But that goes without saying, doesn't it? If you intend to burn through your assets with little regard to your future, I would assume you would not be reading this book in the first place. So, while I am sure you have all your bases covered for the continued upkeep and future procurement of wealth during your lifetime, it is time to look beyond that timeframe. This includes choosing the best options for your heirs and beneficiaries to ensure that you leave them in good hands when you die. Different people want different things for the loved ones they leave behind. How you would like for your heirs to spend or not to spend your money after you pass is irrelevant; what matters is that you leave behind what you want to, and then structure it in a way that suits your vision for the future of your wealth and holdings. While this number (usually around 25 percent of your net worth) is not likely to be used outside of extreme scenarios, that does not mean that you should develop a nonchalant attitude towards it; it's quite the contrary, in fact.

The million-dollar question (quite literally) then becomes, "What is the most efficient way to hold, invest, and ultimately pass these assets down to your heirs?" That is a loaded question for reasons that are tangible and for other reasons that are a bit more emotional and psychological. Let's put on our tweed jackets and examine the psychological angle first. To put it bluntly, most people do not like being faced with their own mortality. While most of my clients have wills and trusts (or should have), at the end of the day, these are merely documents. When it comes to what we view as our money and assets, please recall the assertion most of my clients make that *all* of it is theirs. It's a little harder to come to terms with the truth about our mortality and give in to the fact that sometimes it's necessary to let go a little bit. Understandably, this is not easy for many people. Another psychological factor comes from the fact that we have an innate urge to protect the ones we love. Death changes the ones we leave behind, and whether deliberately or inadvertently, not always for the better. Emotions run high, and the gift of large sums of wealth left behind may cause erratic behaviors. Sadly, although we will be long gone, it is not comforting to imagine that the assets we intended to leave behind might be squandered and frittered away by our heirs.

As I mentioned previously, the three things that most of our clients have in common, perhaps the only three things, is their concern about what we call *CIC* — cost, income, and most importantly, control. Almost any time we work with an affluent client (and most of our clients fall in that category), we pay attention to these issues. What is this going to cost me? How will it affect my income now and in the future? How do I retain control of the situation? Close your eyes… does that sound familiar?

Perhaps the most tangible issue surrounding how we competently invest and hold our assets for our progeny and other heirs comes down to time. If we knew precisely when the assets were to be passed on, planning would be easier. Although my clients pay me well for my erudite planning, I am not Nostradamus, and I cannot predict what the future holds. If I could, I would have bumped Jeff Bezos off the richest person in the world list, and Warren Buffett would be hanging on my every word instead of me taking great interest in what he's saying and doing financially. Nope, I cannot predict the future, but I can look at the past, consider the present, and devise a shrewd plan to protect my clients' wealth and assets. I can also pen this economic tome on the finer points of estate planning to share my financial adroitness with those of you who may never be able to consult me personally. I digress. One thing to always keep in mind is that as with most sound investment plans, everything comes down to asset allocation. It would be prudent to hold some assets in more aggressive investments and others in more conservative ones, although the allocation you go with will likely be based upon personal preference and your stage of life. Suffice it to say, some of the assets would be in fixed income for most older clients.

To reiterate an earlier example, if I could show you an asset class that guaranteed a 6 percent tax-free return with absolutely no risk to the principal, how much of your bottom-tier assets (those earmarked for your heirs) would you invest? This is the essence of utilizing institutionally priced life insurance as a wealth transfer vehicle and paying the premium, not from your own funds (the top 75 percent of your wealth tower), but from the funds that already belong to your heirs (the bottom 25 percent of your wealth tower). The 75/25 split is a generalization; the actual portion size is up to you.

The Invest in Your Life Strategy, Circa 2022

In 2009, I wrote a book called *Invest in Your Life: Why Wall Street Wants You*. The concept of institutionally priced life insurance as an asset class and wealth transfer conduit is fundamental to the *Invest in Your Life* strategy. While specific life insurance products change and evolve over time, conceptually the idea is still efficient and sound.

When I wrote that book, the most prevalent policies we chose to use for this strategy were called Guaranteed Universal Life Insurance policies. In those contracts, the premiums and ultimate death benefits were contractually guaranteed by the insurance company for the life of the insured regardless of the company's future earnings and mortality experience. Earnings on the cash value in those scenarios were irrelevant as we were only focused on the internal rate of return (IRR) on the death benefit when compared to premiums paid. The goal was to *invest* those premiums in the fixed asset class called life insurance death benefits and compare those returns to other investments that the insured could make for their heirs.

The most impactful change in the life insurance market that has happened over the past twelve years has been a reluctance on the part of insurance companies to make such robust guarantees over long periods of time. If you're guessing that the COVID-19 Pandemic scared the daylights out of the life insurance industry's illustrious underwriters and actuaries, you would be half right…right to the extent that during the beginning of the pandemic, issuance of new, large, life insurance policies came to a screeching halt. It took some time for underwriters to get comfortable with the situation. Considering there has been no indication of a long-term drag on mortality rates, things seem to be getting back to normal. However, actuaries and insurance company executives are still losing sleep because they're not exactly sure what to do with your premium dollars on a large scale. Insurance companies must keep the majority of their general account assets invested in safe, fixed-income vehicles (think high grade government and corporate debt). Currently, the yield they're looking for to commit to extraordinary guarantees in their life insurance death benefits over long periods of time eludes them. Fortunately, this is likely a short-term blip on the insurance radar. In the end, insurance companies are businesses that must answer to their stakeholders. Premiums are king (or queen, to be politically correct), and life insurance companies love big premiums.

My paternal grandfather was a career actuary and was astoundingly intelligent. (He would opine that *intelligent* is a redundant term in describing an actuary.) He served as the chief actuary for the Metropolitan Life Insurance Company in the 1960s. I believe my love for numbers and statistics came from my grandfather, who was known respectfully as Mr. Roth. He had a favorite saying: "The perfume of the premium makes up for the stink of the risk." That idea should certainly apply here. There are major companies that are still offering very attractive guarantees; you just need to know where to find them. In addition, you must manage two very important components to any investment program — expectations and actual results. It has never been more important to understand what you are buying and how to manage your portfolio over time.

Guaranteed Survivorship Life Insurance

Let's take a look at what choices a client in our mature affluent group would have for investing the bottom portion of their wealth tower in life insurance death benefits for their heirs. For the purposes of our example, let's assume our clients are a husband and a wife who are both seventy years old and in reasonably good health. We could set up an irrevocable life insurance trust (ILIT) to own one of the following life insurance policies. (Remember, we will be either gifting the premiums, using our lifetime exemption, or lending the premiums to the ILIT.) In most cases, these funds would be utilized to pay future estate taxes for what amounts *to pennies on the dollar,* but not always. My *Invest in Your Life* Strategy is just an investment strategy for your heirs. What they use the fund for is up to them. The rates of return are compelling.

There are major companies that will still guarantee the premiums and death benefit for the life of the contract. In this case of the seventy-year-old husband and wife, we must use a policy that insures the husband and wife and also pays the death benefit upon the passing of the second spouse (aka, second-to-die life insurance). If we were to acquire a

$10 million death benefit for our hypothetical couple, the premium would be just under $214,000 annually. If these premiums were paid every year out of the funds at the bottom of the wealth tower (as an investment of the assets earmarked for the heirs), the IRR on death benefit to the couple's joint life expectancy of 21.8 years would be approximately 6.25 percent tax free and guaranteed. This is approximately a 10.4 percent taxable equivalent yield assuming a 34 percent tax bracket (and I bet yours is higher). I am pretty financially savvy, and I can't think of any fixed income investment that can offer such a deal. I'm not sure I can think of *any* investment at all that can make a similar offer. This is why I suggest that you take a portion of the money that is destined to go to your heirs anyway and invest the fixed income portion of it into life insurance death benefit.

This is generally when I expect a client to ask, "Ron, can you remind me of what the risk is here? I know there is always risk." And my response is, "The only risk is if you live too long." Then after briefly exhibiting a *deer-caught-in-the-headlights* "of a very large truck" look, the client and I share a laugh. If one or both spouses outlive the current joint mortality expectations, the IRR on death benefit will go down. For instance, if the second death does not occur until age 100, the IRR on death benefit would reduce to 3.71 percent tax free. Still not too shabby considering that the client's children and grandchildren would have almost an extra decade to spend with them. As a matter of fact, for this transaction to have a negative IRR expectation, one or both spouses would have to live to age 116! Even if one of the spouses made it to that great age, their heirs would still get the tax-free benefit of $10 million, however, the IRR would be 0.02 percent. Then again, unless you are Moses, you don't have much to worry about in that regard.

Throughout my career in the life insurance business, I

have always tried to take a personal and estate risk management approach to my presentations and interactions with my clients. The hard sell or *grim reaper* approach to life insurance has never been my way. My clients have always been intelligent and perceptive enough to make informed decisions. Woefully, people die in life before they are expected to or are supposed to according to actuarial tables. Actuarial tables are funny things; they can forecast with great accuracy how many people — over long periods of time in a given population — will die each year. However, they will have no clue *who* those people will be. In the *Invest in Your Life* transaction, there is a balance to the downside or the risk of living too long and having lower IRR on death benefit expectations: Some people will die short of their projected life expectancy. In these cases, their heirs will receive rates of return on investment that will be significantly higher than they would have been at expected mortality. In the above example, if the second death occurred at age eighty-eight instead of ninety-nine, the IRR on the death benefit to the heirs would jump from 6.25 percent tax free to just over 9.5 percent tax free. While no one wants to lose a loved one earlier than would be expected for this, it is essential that our clients are informed as to the entire universe of possibilities associated with such a strategy.

The above structure is clearly the safest way to utilize our *Invest in Your Life* strategy because the insurance contract is fully guaranteed for life. There are clients that utilize a strategy in which we only insure one life. The reason they would choose this option is either because there is only one insured available (the second spouse is already deceased, is uninsurable, or there is a divorce situation), or they are looking for a higher rate of return from the strategy.

Individual Guaranteed Universal Life

By utilizing a policy that involves a single life to be insured, we can increase IRR on death benefit to projected mortality upwards of 10 to 13 percent tax free, but this can only fully guarantee coverage to approximately age ninety at this time. That doesn't mean that coverage will end at that point. Instead, as we get closer to projected mortality, we will need to increase premiums (thereby reducing IRR to a certain extent) to ensure that coverage will be in force for the lifetime of the insured. While these structures need to be monitored more closely (annually at a minimum), they are certainly attractive and should never get to a point where there is a negative expected IRR on death benefit unless the insured lives long past age 100.

At age seventy, a male who is in reasonably good health has an empirical life expectancy of just under thirteen more years. The annual premium on $10 million of death benefit would be just over $290,000 annually. If these premiums were paid every year (again, paid out of the funds at the bottom of the wealth tower), the IRR on death benefit to his life expectancy of 12.8 years would be approximately 13.25 percent tax free. This is approximately a 20 percent taxable equivalent yield assuming a 34 percent tax bracket.

At age seventy, a female who also is in good health has an empirical life expectancy of over fifteen years. The annual premium on $10 million of death benefit would be just over $255,000 annually. If these premiums were paid every year (again, paid out of the bottom of the wealth tower), the IRR on death benefit to her life expectancy of 15.36 years would be approximately 9.7 percent tax free. This is approximately a 14.5 percent taxable equivalent yield, assuming a 34 percent tax bracket. As you can see, the IRR on death benefit is lower for a female (assuming the same age and health) than for a male in this scenario even though they are paying less in premiums. This may seem counterintuitive, but when you realize that the premium is being paid for a longer duration because of their increased life expectancy, the equation makes sense. Either way, given the fixed nature of the asset class, this can be a very attractive investment for the heirs, especially when you realize that you are investing their money anyway!

Think of these strategies as a way of using life insurance as an investment. You're gifting the excess of the wealth tower, those bottom-of-the-barrel funds, to fund the ILIT. Another way to think of it is you are loaning your excess from the wealth tower to fund the ILIT. Yes, you lose control, but look at the benefits.

If you are contemplating purchasing a new life insurance policy, be sure to discuss the use of an irrevocable life insurance trust (ILIT) with your advisors before you purchase the policy. Since an ILIT is an irrevocable trust, it is typically used to benefit your spouse and your children by holding the policy proceeds in trust after your death. The main reason people create an ILIT is for the estate tax savings it makes possible. If you die owning the policy, the policy proceeds would be included in your estate and taxed for estate tax purposes. The current federal estate tax exemption is $11.7 million (adjusted yearly for inflation and will be $12.06 million in 2022). If your assets exceed that amount, your estate will be taxed on your death.

Keep in mind that the current $11.7 million exemption amount is scheduled to drop to $5 million (adjusted for inflation) on December 31, 2025. It may drop sooner to an even lower amount now that the Democrats control the White House and Congress. Even if your estate is not federally taxable, your estate may be subject to estate taxes levied by your state of residence. Massachusetts, for example, taxes estates in excess of $1 million. The use of an ILIT could allow your estate to save on estate taxes levied by your state, and that could result in more monies directed to your beneficiaries.

In addition to potential estate tax savings, the use of a trust would allow your trustee to use the policy proceeds for your beneficiaries without giving them full control. This is important if your children are too young at the time of your death to handle the funds appropriately, if you have a second marriage, or if your beneficiaries would not be able to manage the monies successfully on their own.

Here are three things you need to know when you are considering investing in an ILIT.

Select a trustee: It is best to have an independent trustee such as a bank or trust company, or a lawyer or an accountant, but you could also consider a trusted family member or friend. Your spouse could be a co-trustee, and in some instances, they could be the sole trustee. However, if your spouse is the sole trustee, the distributions that he or she could make would be restricted to distributions for health, education, maintenance, and support.

Make sure you understand all the rules: An ILIT requires yearly maintenance and will need to be administered properly. Once the ILIT is signed, you will need to obtain a tax identification number for the trust (typically handled by your attorney). The ILIT is a separate entity apart from you, so it needs its own taxpayer number. The ILIT will then apply for and purchase the life insurance policy. Once the policy is in place, you may not pay the premium directly. You will need to make gifts or loans to the trust. Let's take a look at those options.

Gifting as a Way of Funding the ILIT

As you may be aware, the easiest way to move assets out of your estate is to gift them to someone. The annual gift tax exclusion amount an individual can gift without tax consequences in 2021 was $15,000 to an individual and $30,000 to a married couple. For example, a married couple could each gift up to $90,000 annually to their three children ($30,000 to each child) without any tax consequences. If an individual (the donor) gifts more than the annual gift tax exclusion amount in any one year to another individual, then the excess of the exclusion amount reduces the donor's lifetime gift and estate tax exemption amount (which was $11.7 million in 2021). Though taxes are not required to be paid on the gift amount, a gift tax return must be filed. If the donor depletes their lifetime gift and estate tax exemption amount, then the excess amount over the annual gift tax exclusion is subject to the gift tax.

In some scenarios that involve individuals with excess assets, they may desire to use up all their gift and estate tax credit during their lifetime by making annual gifts valued more than the annual gift tax exclusion. An example of this would be if they gifted their children an amount equal to the annual gift tax exclusion plus the gift and estate tax exemption within a single year. While this amount would not incur any taxation, it would fully use up their allowed gift and estate tax exemption. Then when the individual dies, all their remaining assets in their estate would be subject to estate tax while ignoring any potential increase in the lifetime estate exemption amount in future years.

The decision for an individual to use up their estate tax credit during their lifetime versus at their death — a significant distinction — is often dependent upon whether that individual holds asset they expect to appreciate substantially before their life ends. Should you expect an asset to appreciate rapidly, it is typically better to gift it now at a lower value, even if the gift uses up the estate tax credit. The idea of immediately gifting the assets expected to appreciate the most rapidly in the future is no minor consideration for most gifting strategies; this includes annual gifts that make use of the annual gift tax exclusion. If reducing your taxable estate at the time of your death is a primary goal of your estate plan, then it will likely be to your benefit to make gifts that will allow you to gift someone the broadest amount of potential appreciation in the future.

For example, assume you hold a money market fund worth $200,000 that yields 5 percent annually but does not appreciate; you also have stock worth $200,000 with no dividend yield, but it's expected to appreciate 10 percent each year. From one of these, you wish to make a $200,000 gift to a child. Should you gift the stock or the money market fund? If you gift the money market fund and then die ten years later, the stock would have grown to $518,750, and all that value would be included in your estate. If you gift the stock instead of the money market fund and then die ten years later, the money market fund plus all accrued interest would have grown to approximately $325,780, all of which would be included in your estate. By gifting the stock instead of the money market fund, the value of your estate would be $192, 970 less. That incremental value would belong to your child without being subject to estate taxes.

The future is often as irresolute as our plans for it are. However, that does not mean you cannot make practical and reasonable predictions regarding your assets. In fact, this is imperative for this strategy to work. In larger sample sizes regarding total time, stocks (in general) can be counted on to appreciate faster than bonds. However, in other cases, it can become more complex. While it is true that stocks may generally rise, a specific stock in a certain company may fall. Smaller companies and family businesses that have otherwise proliferated rapidly may abruptly face unforeseen setbacks and losses, thus losing value. Even the most bulletproof gifting strategies can be trumped by a business's cyclical life and death in a price-controlled economy.

Income taxes are also a vital cog in the machine that we call gifting strategy. All your assets receive a step-up in their tax basis regarding their value upon the date of your death. This is done to help determine future capital gains. For example, if you bought a specific stock at $50,000, and it has since grown to $150,000 in value, you will realize $100,000 of capital gains income subject to capital gains tax. However, should you pass away while holding the stock in your name, and your beneficiaries subsequently sell it for $150,000, they will realize no capital gains income upon the sale since it would be treated as if they had paid the full $150,000 for the stock. Conversely, had you gifted the stock to your beneficiaries during your lifetime, they would take over your tax basis in the stock to determine the gain. Should they decide to sell this stock for $150,000 after having been gifted it from you as a lifetime gift, they would realize $100,000 in capital gains income which is subject to capital gains tax.

Upon reading the preceding strategies, you might conclude that individuals with shorter life expectancies and highly appreciated assets may decide not to gift their highly appreciated assets, but instead, retain them in their estates. In effect, this would minimize income taxes, and the individuals could gift other assets with little to no unrealized capital gains instead.

Using another approach, individuals with a long-life expectancy and highly appreciated assets could choose to gift their highly appreciated assets to their beneficiaries who were currently in a significantly lower tax bracket. An example of this would be gifting these assets to grandchildren who could not earn significant income and who could subsequently sell these assets without having to pay any (or comparatively small) capital gains taxes.

Intra-Family Loans

The second strategy in this chapter is an intra-family loan. While gifting assets is a sound strategy, simply put, not everyone wants to make an outright gift and lose control of the $11.7 million per person or $23.4 million per couple lifetime gift and tax exemption amount. A direct result of the Federal Reserve Bank's recent stimulus and interest rate decreases in response to the COVID-19 is the strategy to use intra-family loans to transfer wealth to future generations with zero gift tax consequences and the ability to renegotiate already existing intra-family loans at reduced interest rates.

A positive attribute of this strategy is that it requires a relatively low cost to implement. According to the Internal Revenue code, making loans to relatives at far lower rates charged by commercial lenders, without classifying them as a gift, is perfectly legal. To avoid the loan being classified as a gift, the lender, who is typically a parent or grandparent, must charge interest to the borrower. This interest is called the applicable federal rate or the AFR. The loan recipient, who is typically a child or grandchild, must earn a greater return on the amount borrowed than the AFR. Understanding this, the interest rate may be as low as 0.99 percent on a loan term of three to nine years with interest being paid annually. As of July 2021, the rates range from 1 percent to 2.07 percent. Another positive characteristic of this type of loan is that the lender can structure it so that the borrower only pays the interest during the loan term, and then only repays the principle upon the end of the term. However, should a parent or grandparent grant an interest-free loan to a child or grandchild, the IRS would treat all foregone interest as a taxable gift. This might also include simply forgiving the loan at the end of its term.

An example of this strategy in action would be the following scenario. If a grandparent grants their grandchild a 9-year loan of $3 million, the loan could only be considered a successful estate planning tool if the grandchild would earn over 0.99 percent with the money they borrowed. Let's say the grandchild invests the $3 million for the entire 9-year period at a 6 percent annual rate of return. That grandchild would have $5,068,437 at the end of the loan term andwould only have to repay the grandparent $3,278,133 throughout the entirety of the course of the loan. Therefore, the grandchild could keep the $1,790,304 difference, negating any gift tax consequences.

While intra-family loans assuredly have beneficial attributes for the transfer of wealth to future generations, there are other positive aspects as well. These loans can be much kinder than those from third-party lenders since the total interest paid over the lifetime of the loan stays within the family as opposed to being paid to the bank. For those would-be lenders whose progeny have poor credit, this affords them the funds necessary for buying a home or starting a business. This arrangement is easier on both the lender and borrower because no one is responsible for the superfluous administration costs, closing costs, and appraisal fees that are commonplace with standard loans.

CHAPTER 5

Private Placement Life Insurance

To this point in our journey, we have shared with you some interesting techniques to acquire substantial amounts of life insurance for planning purposes. Whether the goal was to protect your family, business, or estate, we detailed a clear need to buy life insurance, or we demonstrated how using life insurance *death benefit* could be a valuable investment for your heirs using our *Invest in Your Life* strategy.

We now move on to a strategy in which the death benefit, while important, is only *a part* of this strategy's attraction. In most cases, this strategy looks to buy *as little* life insurance as possible. Does this sound strange coming from someone in the high-end life insurance business for the past thirty years? Maybe. But read on.

Fortunately, this a surprisingly simple strategy that could potentially save you and your family millions of dollars from the hands of the government. Legal experts have called this strategy "*a massive loophole — entirely legal, easy to exploit, and politically very hard to close," (Source www.bloomberg.com/2021-09-02).*

This strategy is called *Private Placement Life Insurance* (PPLI), an exclusive type of insurance only offered to qualified wealthy individuals. PPLI is often used as a tax-exempt way to generate income and grow wealth in addition to providing a way to leave a substantial financial estate to your family.

To properly understand how a PPLI policy might fit into your portfolio and why so many wealthy Americans are seizing this opportunity, we first need to review life insurance policies as a whole. Let's jump right in and start with the basics.

Life Insurance: The Basics

At its most rudimentary form, life insurance is a transactional policy where you pay a fee (a "premium") to an insurance company, and in return, your loved ones receive some amount of money (the "death benefit") after you pass away.

The cost of life insurance premiums is calculated based on three factors: (1) your life expectancy based on your age, health, and family history; (2) the dollar amount of your death benefit; and (3) the length of coverage or how long your policy will last.

Permanent vs. Term Life Insurance

The two primary forms of life insurance are *permanent* and *term*. As the names imply, a permanent life insurance policy covers an individual for their entire life, while a term policy only covers that individual for a predetermined number of years (usually ten, but it can be as little as five or as great as forty years).

Term life insurance policies tend to be cheaper but carry a significant risk. With a term policy, you pay premiums for the duration of that term, and your family will receive the death benefit if — and only if — you pass away within that term.

Let's say you're fifty years old, and you take out a 10-year term life insurance policy. The day you turn sixty, you are no longer covered, and every penny you paid to the insurance company is now nothing more than padding on their balance sheet. If you wanted to continue coverage at the end of the term, you would need to start a brand-new policy with a much higher premium since your life expectancy would then be ten years shorter.

On the other hand, permanent life insurance covers you for your entire life. There is no possibility of losing your coverage and leaving your family out in the cold. This basic premise makes permanent life insurance a superior alternative to term even if it is more costly initially. With a permanent life insurance policy, you pay extra into the policy upfront when your liability is low to receive a discount on your more expensive years later in life.

While permanent life charges higher premiums in the early years of your policy than is needed, this additional funding creates a surplus of cash (the "cash value") within the account. The cash value then becomes an asset that can be invested at interest over time. In addition, ***due to the favorable tax treatment of life insurance, this investment grows tax free within the life insurance policy and can be accessed during your life on a tax-favored basis as well. I can see the light bulbs going off already...***

Variable Life Insurance

Variable life insurance is a subset of permanent life insurance, with others including whole and universal life. Each type of permanent life insurance policy is essentially defined by how the cash value of the policy can be invested.

With whole life insurance, your money is invested into low-risk, low-reward, investment vehicles (like CDs) which can grow tax-deferred over time. While offering safety and stability, whole life policies leave much to be desired in terms of rate of return.

On the other hand, the cash value of a variable life insurance policy is placed in a separate account that is considered by the U.S. Securities and Exchange Committee to be the property of the life insurance company. (Keep this in mind as we'll return to this concept later.) Because the cash value is considered the property of the insurance company, the capital gains appreciated by the policy are tax exempt.

These funds can be placed in any investment offered by the insurance company and usually include a menu of assets including stocks, bonds, mutual funds, and alternative investments such as gold, real estate, and hedge funds.

While there is additional risk involved in a variable life policy, anyone arguing for whole life over variable life would be like your financial advisor suggesting you place your entire 401(k) in a basic savings account. That advisor should be fired…and fast.

The only drawback of basic variable life insurance is that the investment options are limited by what is offered by the insurance company, thus reducing your choices as the policyholder.

Enter: Private Placement Life Insurance.

Private Placement Life Insurance

PPLI is nothing new; in fact, it was first developed in the 1970s. But given what you already know about the changing nature of taxation of the wealthy in this country, it's no surprise that PPLI is back in the limelight (much to the dismay of Uncle Sam). This is especially impactful since for the past five decades this product has operated primarily to move taxable investments into a tax-free environment. It's a quite effective and discretionary environment to boot.

PPLI can only be offered to qualified, select, *high and* ultra-high net worth *individuals,* and has been called the *Rich Man's Roth IRA* due to the myriad tax advantages and guarantees these policies offer.

How Private Placement Life Insurance is Structured

INVESTIMENTS

- Ria Controlled
- Hedge Fund Partnerships
- Real Estate
- Private Equity
- Business Interests
- IPO Investments

Pure Life Insurance Benefit
Net Amount At Risk

The investments made in PPLI policies use a structure called insurance-dedicated funds (IDFs) which allow the product to offer mirror-image funds of any investable fund available to the public. This is similar in nature to how exchange-traded funds (ETFs) are structured. In addition, many structures allow policyholders to have their current investment managers accredited for the product, thereby changing little to none of their current investment strategy—other than the taxation. Further, these IDFs allow the cash value of your life insurance policy to be invested in an effectively unlimited scope of investment vehicles of *your choosing,* allowing your money to grow to its greatest potential.PPLI policies can act as a source of tax-free income since you are allowed to withdraw as much money as you like from the fund up to the total amount of premiums you have paid into it (your basis) without incurring a single cent of capital gains or income taxes. After that amount is withdrawn, you can access policy funds by using very inexpensive policy loans where you are effectively paying interest back to yourself.

What about the death benefit?

In most scenarios, the death benefit will include all investments and growth in the policy. Most of our clients structure these policies in an irrevocable trust for estate planning and distribution purposes.

Tax Advantages of PPLI

Private placement life insurance allows for the cash value of your life insurance policy to grow tax free with no capital gains or ordinary income taxes. Next, withdrawals from the cash value of your account by loan will not trigger any income taxes either. Lastly, the death benefits your loved ones receive is paid out tax free regardless of the beneficiary.

In addition, the IDF structure of PPLI policies combined with the ability to invest in a variety of alternative assets, allows for tax-deferred or tax-exempt investment in otherwise highly tax-inefficient vehicles such as real estate investment trusts and hedge funds.

Contribution Limits

Comparable to variable annuities, PPLI policies do not have any defined annual contribution limits. So, you could theoretically contribute an unlimited amount into the policy. The only caveat is that there must be enough total death benefit (relative to the cash/investment value) so the plan still qualifies as life insurance under the tax code. We are able to ensure that PPLI structures maintain compliance with these regulations because we monitor them closely as the investments grow over time.

Investor Control Doctrine

Now that you know that you can invest as much as you want and in whatever investments you want with essentially no contribution limits, income taxes, or capital gains taxes, you may be wondering, "What's the catch, Ron?"

Fair question.

The catch is that PPLI policies can only be considered tax exempt due to a legal requirement called the *Investor Control Doctrine.* This rule prohibits you as the policyholder from directly selecting or indirectly influencing the selection of assets within the policy's portfolio once the policy has been set in motion.

Do you recall back to when we discussed that the cash value of the insurance policy is technically owned by the insurance company? This is the legal distinction that allows you to avoid paying hefty capital gains and income taxes. The *Investor Control Doctrine* was put in place to ensure that this arrangement was the true nature of the policy and not just a cloak used for tax shielding- purposes.

However, according to *Webber v. Commissioner of Internal Revenue* (2015), the presiding Judge Lauber ruled that the policyholder is permitted to make "broad suggestions" to the IDF manager. Remember, in most cases you choose the IDF manager for your private placement policy.

Diversification Requirements Under Section 817(h)(1)

As a final regulatory measure, private placement life insurance policies also need to be considered adequately diversified to qualify as life insurance policies according to Section 817(h)(1). This Section states that the portfolio of a life insurance policy cannot hold more than the following:

1. 55 percent of the total asset value in any one investment.
2. 70 percent of the total asset value in any two investments.
3. 80 percent of the total asset value in any three investments.
4. 90 percent of the total asset value in any four investments.

Comparable to IRS rules surrounding tax loss harvesting techniques, assets that are considered "substantially identical" may be considered the same asset for the purpose of measuring diversification within your policy.

It is important for you and your trusted financial advisor to realize that the diversification qualification must be met at the beginning of the policy and throughout the life of the policy. With such strict requirements, periodic rebalancing will be a necessity.

Considerations When Selecting a PPLI Partner

Given the bespoke nature of PPLI in the insurance world, it is not unusual that many insurance agents and financial advisors have limited knowledge of how these policies can be effectively used as investments with significant tax advantages to wealthy individuals like yourself.

Due to the legal complexities and potential risks associated with PPLI policies, it's essential to work with a partner consisting of experts in financial, legal, actuarial, and risk-management fields to keep you out of hot water with the IRS.

A Review of the Benefits of PPLI

- PPLI provides the ability to grow previously taxable assets in a tax-free environment.
- It offers access to withdraw funds up to your basis on a tax-free basis at no cost, and then the ability to make tax-free loans from the plan at rates as low as thirty basis points.
- It affords flexibility to use your current investment managers.
- It delivers the ability to shield IPO gains from taxes.
- PPLI can also be a very efficient repository to shield "low value" stock which may realize a tremendous gain in the future.

Chapter 6

Captive Insurance

I'm going to go out on a limb and assume that many of you, maybe most of you, either own your own business or are a partner in a business or professional practice. Whatever the nature of that business or practice is, it has operating costs. And, if you're like most of my clients, commercial insurance premiums are one of the highest costs of doing business. Absolutely nobody enjoys paying the expenses on those policies since these are expenses over which they often feel they have little to no control. This fact is as relevant as ever as I write this book in late 2021 during the COVID-19 Pandemic. However, even before the pandemic, the commercial insurance market was widely regarded as in a *hard market* because commercial insurance premiums had steadily increased for over ten consecutive quarters. To further compound this issue, the top commercial insurance brokers in the country don't currently offer any readily available solutions.

However, my colleagues and I have a solution: Set up your own insurance company.

I'm not being facetious. As I discussed earlier in this book, I'm hauntingly aware of the insurance industry's checkered past and reputation. I would wager that many of you are accustomed to being presented with sophisticated investment plans, not something involving insurance. You're probably wondering why on earth would you become involved in all the rigamarole involved in owning an insurance company. You have plenty of insurance already — for your business-healthcare, cars, etc. Put aside your preconceived ideas and hear me out. Owning your own insurance company may not be something you ever considered doing, but it's a strategy that is tried and true and endorsed by none other than Warren Buffett. Yes, Warren Buffett, also known as the Oracle of Omaha, is considered the most successful investor of the twentieth century and was worth an estimated $100.3 billion in March 2021 according to *Forbes* magazine; he buys insurance companies. Warren Buffett is known for being extremely frugal. He will drive a car until his daughter tells him it's so tatty it's embarrassing. He lives in the same Omaha house he bought in 1958, and he doesn't take lavish vacations. If Warren Buffett is spending money to buy insurance companies, you can rest assured it's a good place for an investor to be. Now why, with all the investment opportunities available in things like emerging technology companies, would he be interested in an investment concept that's been around for hundreds of years? Mr. Buffett buys insurance companies for several reasons, but primarily because they have significant tax benefits in addition to the lucrative underwriting profits that can be made in the business.

This is where captive insurance companies come into play.A captive insurance company is merely a private insurance company that only insures the risks of the underlying parent company and is typically owned with the same ownership arrangement as the parent company. The captive insurance company is paid premiums from the parent company, and the captive company covers risks, reinsures risks, and guess what else it does? It makes profits just like any other insurance company. However, unlike commercial insurance companies, this captive setup eliminates a massive layer of expenses typically found in their commercial counterparts. These expenses are embedded in the commercial industry and include marketing, home office expenses, agent commissions, etc. Did you know that approximately 35 percent of your premium goes on to cover insurance company overhead when you pay a commercial insurance company?

Now we can't cover all risks in a captive insurance company. Only the risks that make the most sense based upon an actuarial study can be deemed potentially profitable to the underlying business within question. The fact that 90 percent of Fortune 500 companies own their very own captive insurance companies is a sure sign of this strategy's effectiveness. We can show you how to apply these concepts toward a more mid-market business, which is far more relevant to the vast majority of people who are reading this.

The Foundation

To put it simply, a captive insurance company is an insurance company that is created specifically to serve the needs of a specific business entity. For the purposes of this text, I will focus on *single-parent captives*, but it's important to know other structures exist. The ownership structure of the underlying parent company is generally mirrored in the ownership of the captive insurance company. The parent company funds the captive's loss reserves (a portion of which is either reinsured or pooled with other companies for safety purposes) and controls its operations. Owners work with a consultant or captive manager to develop a thorough understanding of whatever specific risks are associated with the nature of their business. When that is done, the consultant creates a customized policy that actuarially reflects those risks and is priced accordingly. Rather than paying premiums to a commercial insurance carrier, the owners pay premiums to their captive insurer.

The concept of self-insurance may be familiar to you. This type of arrangement occurs when a business or other organization sets aside financial reserves either on its books or within a special bank account to hedge against potential risks. Although it goes much further than that concept, fundamentally, a captive insurance company is a form of self-insurance. It's very important to note here that *all companie*s (including Fortune 500 companies) have some sort of commercial insurance in place. The key to making the concept work is what my colleagues and I call *layering*. Layering establishes which risks should be transferred to a commercial insurer, and which should be self-insured or covered by the captive. Generally, the larger the underlying parent company is, the less the risk is that is required to be transferred. Smaller companies will want to transfer or reinsure a larger portion of their risks, especially those risks that could cause claims of a catastrophic nature. This determination of risk distribution and risk transfer is typically analyzed by having a feasibility study prepared by a captive consultant or captive manager long before a captive insurance company is formed. This feasibility study will determine if the underlying company is a good candidate for a captive, will analyze the specific risks of the company, will project long-term financial benefits of a captive, and will recommend the best alternatives for managing risk efficiently based on the underlying company's industry, operations, and loss history.

A captive insurance company is a licensed and regulated insurance company that must be established within a domicile (state) in compliance with all the laws and regulations of that domicile. This customarily includes a standard for capitalization and reserves, periodic audits, specific actuarial requirements, and captive management. The captive insurance company is a legal entity that is also separate from the business that own it. You would not be mistaken if you recognized similar characteristics between a mutual insurance company and a captive insurance company although there are notable differences. While it is true that its policyholders also own a mutual insurance company, unlike a captive insurance company, they lack control of the insurer. While the policyholders of a mutual insurance company may submit a proxy that approves members of the board of directors, all control is indirect at best. When the insured company ceases making premium payments, they also cease ownership. Although mutual insurance companies are often able to issue dividends after a profitable year, most simply use these profits to bulk up their reserves.

One of the most significant distinctions between captive insurance companies and other approaches is the very nature of the owner's payments to the insurance company. Should your business be covered by a traditional insurance carrier (either an investor-owned company or a mutual company), you pay regular premiums that are classified simply as an expense to your business. After a set period, and once the premiums provided coverage, you would have no more equity remaining. Normally the money you'd pay to a captive insurance company would be classified as a business expense for tax purposes. Your premiums and that of the other group members would become assets of your insurance company's reserves (invested conservatively to provide liquidity) and would be available to pay out any claims. Any surplus funds not immediately needed for claims could then grow through more robust investments. Should the amount of any claims turn out to be less than expected, and the reserves were modestly invested, it is possible that the owner's contributions could be scaled back in future years. This would subsequently enhance the cash flow of your company. To put it differently, rather than transferring your money to a commercial insurance company that would not provide any return on investment, with a captive insurance company, you would not only receive the coverage that you wanted, but you would also put yourself into a position to benefit from any underwriting profit earned by said captive insurance *and* reap significant benefits in the interim.

The Benefits of Owning a Captive Insurance Company

There are several advantages to choosing the captive insurance company approach because it offers significant advantages to its owners. The captive insurance route provides much greater control than its alternatives. Because you own and control this captive insurance company, you determine the rules...within reason and legal limits, of course. You determine the nature of your risk management, essentially setting deductibles, determining policy limits, and maximizing payouts and standards for your claims. Your insurance company may also be able to pay for certain services such as loss control for you and any other owners as an investment in reducing claims.

If you are like most of us, you may hold your breath when renewal time for your insurance policy approaches. If that's the case, then predictable pricing is another benefit that you would enjoy with a captive insurance company. Businesses will often face costly year-over-year premium increases (that often come with little or no warning) from more traditional insurance carriers. That makes it tricky to budget for coverage. However, when you are a captive insurance company owner, you are acutely aware of its financial performance and have a better sense of any upcoming changes. Additionally, if your actuarial guidance and underwriting practices are sound, there is a strong chance that you will see reductions as opposed to increases.

The operating advantages afforded to owners of captive insurance companies are plentiful as well. The sponsoring company can benefit from a much more robust approach to risk management. Specifically, the parent or sponsoring company can formally insure risks that previously may have been uninsured; these include many of the risks highlighted by FEMA on ready.gov.

Another interesting facet of these captive companies is the overall aggregate wealth of a company or companies with a captive insurance company is almost always not just higher, but *significantly* higher than the overall wealth of those companies without a captive insurance company. This is not simply a coincidence. The parent company takes an expense as it pays its insurance premium to its captive, which in turn lowers the parent company's taxable income. The second reason is that the captive can earn a return on investment for its reserve pool (assets), and this asset pool can be expanded with pre-tax dollars, thus creating a much larger starting base for assets to grow. There is no shortage of risks regularly faced by businesses that informally self-insure. Should an event occur, the business would be forced to bite the bullet, often resulting in a loss that could lead to workers being laid off and the business to face partial or total closure. Having captive insurance allows businesses to formally insure risks that would otherwise not be insured by third-party insurers.

As the adage goes, life is not a bowl of cherries, and adverse events will occur regardless of whether a business has a captive insurance company in place or not. Businesses with a captive in place have access to a significantly larger pool of funds to address these adverse events. This isbecause a captive's assets are composed of pre-tax dollars. Thus, the captive effectively serves as a legal tax haven for the premiums received from its insured. These premiums are paid from the sponsoring company to the captive with tax deductible dollars. Depending upon the size of the captive, its premium income is received either fully tax favored (smaller 831b captives) or with large reserve offsets against premium income (831a captives). This tax favored income can be invested by the captive and will only be diminished at some point in the future when the actual claims need to be paid. As you can see, you have the legal opportunity to invest and grow funds which without a captive would have been paid to Uncle Sam. It's no wonder Mr. Buffet likes these so much. Finally, assets of the captive are not available to creditors of the business owner or the underlying business itself, thereby offering asset insulation and protection.

The following graph shows a financial comparison of commercial and private captive insurance companies:

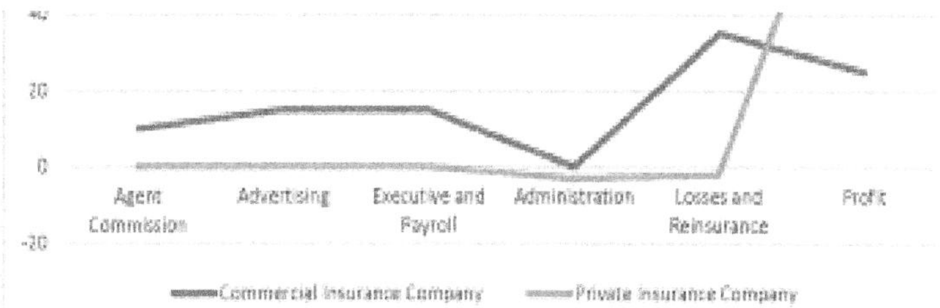

There is no shortage of reasons for the conditions under which captive insurance companies are formed. Oftentimes, companies are unable to obtain necessary insurance coverage, while in other cases, there is a hardening of premiums that drives companies to seek out less expensive coverage. It might be that companies simply want to have more control over their current insurance programs. Regardless of the reasoning behind the choice, the end goal is to produce a compliant entity that will also recognize and abide by the many years of court decisions that have helped to shape the modern, captive insurance industry. As it currently stands, commercial insurance companies are simply not capable of reacting to the rapid changes of the modern marketplace appropriately, nor are they ever truly capable of insuring the numerous hidden risks that most businesses routinely face. Proper risk management requires an integrated commercial and private insurance approach as I illustrate below.

In 2015, a medical practice of considerable size developed a captive insurance company. This medical practice's insurance premiums regarding malpractice were excessively high, so they created a captive for the purpose of developing a "war chest" to fund the deductible costs related to their medical malpractice insurance policy. The design of this captive abided by all rules and regulations of their domicile and contained thirty-four additional lines of insurance coverage. The resulting effect was a substantial reduction in claims against the practice's commercial insurance company. This occurred because of the accumulated assets available to control claims, and because of a behavioral shift in the practice's members who quickly realized that their money was funding the deductibles. As the captive's assets grew, the practice decided to increase the deductibles on the commercial medical malpractice policy. This resulted in lower commercial insurance premiums as the captive took on more of the deductible risk.

Currently, this practice's commercial medical malpractice policy is half of the cost for similar medical groups in its geographic location. Since its inception in 2015, the patients served by the medical malpractice have changed, the local community's demographics have changed, and the passing of the Patient Protection and Affordable Care Act has changed the medical marketplace. The resulting effect was the practice began to see more patients relying on Medicaid. In 2017, Medicaid decided to audit the practice. The time, the legal fees, and the use of staff for reconstructing notes resulted in a substantial cost to the practice. Fortunately, their captive insurance company contained two policies that were designed to assist in this type of disruption: one provided legal protection, and the other covered any audit expenses. Both policies were among a much larger pool of policies so the costs to the practice were manageable. Neither line of coverage would have been available in the commercial marketplace. Still, because of the captive strategy, the medical practice had the ability to choose the attorneys that represented them in the Medicaid audit.

One of the doctors in this practice is considering retirement, and should he decide to resign, his buyout will be partially funded from the assets within the captive. This is an excellent example of how a well-structured captive can change a business for the better while simultaneously serving the community more effectively. The financial stability created by the captive has led to a steady increase in the overall number of employees in the practice, and the staff has gained a greater sense of control and peace of mind. Issues that would have otherwise been threats to the practice's solvency have been resolved in a much smoother way because of the captive.

Successful captives serve a wide array of businesses ranging from large professional practices to manufacturing and distribution businesses. The benefits extend to them all as well. For example, a nursing home in Brooklyn recently experienced a fire that was caused by a patient lighting a cigarette in his room. I have never heard of enjoying a smoke after surgery, but perhaps the next time I'm headed to the

OR, I'll take some cigarettes along and give it the old college try. Anyway, the sprinkler system flooded the building, and the commercial insurance carrier insuring the nursing home covered everything except the front lobby because of an exclusion in the commercial coverage. Luckily, the nursing home had captive insurance which covered this loss.

Most recently, we have seen captive insurance step in to cover losses to businesses due to the COVID-19 Pandemic that were not insured under their commercial policies. Most businesses carry business interruption insurance. If a company is forced to stop doing business due to a warehouse burning down, a flood, or the like, the business can be reimbursed for lost income while the damage is being repaired. Many business owners submitted such claims when they were forced to shut down for a period of time during the COVID-19 quarantine. The vast majority were dismayed to find out that they were not covered for these losses because their commercial policies carried exclusions that required there to be "an underlying physical loss" such a fire or flood for the business interruption insurance to become operational. Most captive insurance had no such exclusions and pandemic losses were covered in many cases.

From modest beginnings, the captive insurance industry has developed into a robust alternative for many businesses across the country. These results are based on the practical risk-management needs of businesses that extend beyond what could be efficiently insured by the commercial market by itself. Captive legislation was born from the congressional belief that insurance, proper capitalization, and proper management are imperative for businesses to operate and grow. Most astute business owners understand the inherent risks their businesses face in their market sector. At the same time, smaller companies do not have the team of in-house advisors that larger companies do, and captive insurance companies somewhat level the playing field by being a viable option for saving costs and growing assets.

CHAPTER 7

Taxes and Traditions

As we have discussed at length as affluent individual in the top 1 percent of earners, you will naturally be a larger target for taxation. It is precisely because of this reason that understanding the tax landscape is of the utmost importance moving forward. In this chapter, we will cover the current tax landscape, the proposed changes, and the history of the estate and capital gains taxes in this country. While there are no guarantees, history can be an excellent trove of knowledge to use in predicting or preparing for the future.

Joining the ranks of the top 1 percent of earners and wealth holders in the country implies that you have uncommon proficiency in some income-earning endeavours, which very likely requires a strong understanding and intimate knowledge of specific concepts and strategies within that field. Regardless of what that field or industry is, you have earned enough income and/or accumulated enough assets to be within the top 1 percent. Keeping that in mind, I want to help you apply those same principles of understanding and knowledge required to excel in your field to the retention of your wealth. Even among the truly rich, there is turnover.

For example, in 1982, *Forbes* magazine ran its first list of the 400 richest Americans. That list included fourteen members of the Rockefeller family, twenty-eight members of the du Pont family, and eleven members of the Hunt family. That same list twenty years later included only three members of the Rockefeller family, one member of the Hunt family, and no members of the du Pont family. It's not what you expected, is it? Within a single year, the nation's 400 richest people lost a collective $283 billion in net worth, which among a host of other reasons, was a contributing factor in the turnover.

The wealthiest, brightest, and most established among

us are not impervious to losing wealth. I do not intend to use scare tactics or make my tone too ominous. I only intend to use my words as a sobering reminder that change is inevitable, and while some circumstances are out of our control, we nevertheless must do our best to arm ourselves to the teeth with knowledge. You cannot protect your wealth if you fail to pay attention to the harbingers of change.

With that being said, bear with me during this chapter. I will do my best to be concise, transparent, and humorous; perhaps I will be so funny you will forget you are reading about boring old taxes. Let's be real; my humor may be so bad that you might shake your head and laugh in amazement that someone would put it into print. With either scenario, you are being distracted from an otherwise stodgy subject, so I will chalk it up as a win for the both of us.

Why Am I being Taxed?

According to the Tax Policy Center, roughly 9 percent of the households in the United States have incomes higher than $200,000, and they receive almost 45 percent of all pre-tax income. And then there are the *really* rich, who are in the top percent of households — about 700,000 in all — that have incomes above $1 million a year and collect about 13 percent of all pre-tax income.

Since the 1980s, those at the very top have enjoyed faster growing incomes than the rest of America. The Congressional Budget Office (CBO) estimates that the upper echelons of the American 1 percent (average annual income $1.8 million in 2016) saw their inflation-adjusted incomes before taxes nearly *triple* between 1979 and 2016. The top 9 percent saw theirs grow by 75 percent while everyone else saw their pre-tax incomes rise by 33 percent.

Despite what some talking heads and politicians might purport, the rich generally pay more of their incomes toward taxes than the rest of the country. According to the CBO, the top fifth of American households generated 54 percent of all income and yet paid 69 percent of federal taxes; the top 1 percent made 16 percent of the income and paid 25 percent of all federal taxes. The incomes of the top 20 percent rose faster than those of the rest of the population. The after-tax-and-transfers income of the top 1 percent rose by 226 percent between 1979 and 2016; this is nearly five times faster than the incomes of people in the middle of the income distribution rose.

Let's discuss the various types of tools Uncle Sam has at his disposal to tax you. And while this may be known to most of you, it's important to reiterate the basics. It also gets a bit dry…think Sahara. So, for those of you who want to dispense with the history, I won't be offended if you skip this section.

A Brief History of Capital Gains

A capital gains tax is a tax imposed on the increase in the value of an investment when people or companies sell it. The capital gains are said to have been *realized* when the assets are sold. Unsold investments or *unrealized capital gains* are exempt from the tax collector. Therefore, stock shares that appreciate year after year will not be subject to capital gains taxes unless they are sold, regardless of how long they are owned. Furthermore, the capital gains tax in the United States only applies to long-term capital gains or income on the sale of assets kept for over one year. In addition, depending on an individual's tax bracket, the rates may range from 0 percent to 15 percent, then up to slightly more than 20 percent. Ultimately, short-term capital gains are taxed as ordinary income and apply to assets held for less than a year.

In 1913, the U.S. government implemented the first-ever capital gains tax. The Sixteenth Amendment to the Constitution gave Congress the authority to impose income taxes. Congress introduced the first income tax in October of that year. The government set the tax rate at 1 percent for those making less than $500,000 per year. For those earning more, they set the rate at a whopping 7 percent. This was far from the first time (and certainly not the last time) that the government would impose a higher tax on the affluent. Three short years later, the government hiked up the minimum income tax rate by 2 percent while those earning more than $1.5 million had their rate increased to 15 percent. For the next few years, Congress would continue this onerous game of tug-of-war, going as far as implementing an early form of estate tax during a time of conflict although it was repealed once the dust had cleared. This all changed with the Revenue Act of 1916 which we will get to shortly.

The Effects of Capital Gains Tax

Capital gains taxes beget the benefit of deferring tax payments until an asset is sold. For example, a real estate investor does not have to pay taxes on the equity generated in an investment property until they sell it for a profit. Likewise, when a securities investor receives a pay out or sells assets, capital gains taxes are not due on earnings gained from stocks and bonds. Investors only pay taxes during the year in which they make a profit. This stipulation differs from income taxes, which require individuals to pay a tax on all wages reported to the IRS.

Nearly everything an individual owns for personal use or investment purposes is categorized as a capital asset by the Internal Revenue Service. Owning capital assets has the disadvantage of requiring individuals and corporations to record profits as income if the assets are sold for a profit. Ultimately, this tax has the disadvantage of reducing the overall earnings realized from the asset sale.

Tax Rates

The tax rate an individual must pay on a capital gain is determined by how long they have held the asset prior to selling it; this can be beneficial or harmful to the taxpayer depending upon the circumstances under which they sell it. Suppose an individual possesses an asset for longer than a year before selling it. The profit made on that investment would be considered a long-term capital gain; this in turn would be taxed at a reduced rate. Conversely, a short-term capital gain occurs when an asset is owned for less than twelve months and is subsequently sold for a profit. In that case, the capital gain would be subject to a higher rate. Because the rate is lower, long-term capital gains taxes are preferable to short-term capital gains taxes.

Long-term capital gains tax rates as of 2018 range from 0 percent to 20 percent depending on the taxpayer's tax group. For example, those in the 10 percent and 15 percent tax brackets pay no long-term capital gains tax, whereas those in the 39.6 percent bracket pay the full 20 percent. Individuals can counterbalance capital gains of up to $3,000 in ordinary income with tax losses. If they are selling stock to take advantage of a tax loss, they would want to avoid buying it again within thirty days, or the IRS would deny the loss under their wash sale rules.

In many situations, the responsibility for reporting federal and state capital gains taxes fall on the taxpayers. The majority of states require property owners and investors to record capital gains upon the sale of real estate on both state and federal income tax returns. Be that as it may, the state's additional tax — or double tax — is a disadvantage.

Capital Gains Tax Attributes

When an individual or an organization sells an asset or investment for less than the price they initially paid, they incur capital losses. Capital losses from investments can mitigate taxes on capital gains. Capital losses, like gains, appear in short-term and long-term forms and must be offset by capital gains of the equivalent type first. If individuals have long-term capital losses, they must first utilize them to balance any long-term capital gains. After that, taxpayers can use any remaining losses to offset short-term capital gains. They can also offset up to $3,000 of other income such as earnings or dividends with capital losses. Unused capital losses can get carried over to subsequent tax years.

There are exceptions to capital gains taxes, and different regulations apply to different types of capital gains. Capital gains from the sale of collectibles such as art, antiques, and precious metals, as well as owner-occupied real estate, are among the most notable examples. Individuals who realize long-term capital gains from the sale of collectibles including precious metals, coins, or artwork, face a maximum tax rate of 28 percent. Short-term capital gains on collecting assets are nevertheless subject to ordinary income taxation. The IRS divides collectible assets into different classes.The following is a list of those classes:

- Alcoholic beverages such as valuable vintage wines
- Musical instruments and historical objects
- Stamps and coins
- Works of art, rugs, and antiques
- Precious metals and gems

It is important to note that the IRS considers precious metals to be collectibles. With that being the case, it's important to note that long-term capital gains from the sale of shares in any pass-through investment vehicle that engages in precious metals, like an exchange-traded fund or mutual fund, are normally taxed at a rate of 28 percent.

Capital Gains Tax Lowered

In a variety of ways, legislation has cut capital gains taxes on investors. For example, the maximum marginal long-term capital gains tax rate was reduced from 28 percent to 20 percent, while the 15 percent bracket was lowered to 10 percent. Legislation also increased the amount of time a taxpayer must hold an item eligible for lower long-term capital gains tax rates from twelve months to eighteen months.

In 2020, the government set these long-term capital gains tax rates at 0 percent, 15 percent, and 20 percent, with the rate being dependent upon the individual taxpayer's incomelevel. Likewise, short-term capital gains are now taxed at thefiler's regular income tax rate. For this situation, the term *short-term* refers to something with a duration of less than one year.

Any capital gains realized upon the disposal of a private residence up to $500,000 for married couples filing jointlyan $250,000 for single individuals became exempt from taxation under the 1997 Act. However, this exemption has only been available to taxpayers who have lived in their homes for at least two of the previous five years. Furthermore, this benefit can only be claimed every two years for those who qualify.

To recap: capital gains tax is a tax levied on the rise in the value of an investment when an individual or business sells it. When these assets are sold, the capital gains are deemed to be *realized*. Conversely, any unrealized capital gains or unsold assets are free from tax. Therefore, stock shares that appreciate year after year would not be liable to capital gains taxes unless they were sold, regardless of how long they were owned. In the United States, the capital gains tax only applies to long-term capital gains, or revenue derived from the sale of assets held for more than a year. Additionally, depending on an individual's tax category, rates can be as low as 0 percent to 15 percent, or as high as 20 percent. Short-term capital gains which apply to assets held for less than a year are taxed as ordinary income.

The 2017 Tax Cuts and Jobs Act (TCJA) has kept the favorable tax rates on long-term capital gains and the 3.8 percent net interest income tax (NIIT). For taxpayers with higher incomes, the TCJA splits the tax rate thresholds for capital gains from the tax rates for regular income. The income levels for the new capital gains tax tiers continue to be updated for inflation, while the NIIT income levels are not since they are under previous law. The TCJA has also repealed the phaseout of itemized deductions, which in some cases has increased the maximum capital gains tax rate over the 23.8 percent statutory rate.

Long-term capital gains have been taxable at lower rates than regular income for almost the entirety of the history of income taxation. For example, from 1988 to 1990, the highest long-term capital gains and ordinary income tax rates were the same. Qualified dividends have also gotten taxed at a lower rate since 2003. Today, to avoid being stung by a projected U.S. capital gains tax rate, wealth planners advise clients to max out their retirement accounts, park their earnings in tax-deferred opportunity zone funds, and even liquidate some assets. The Biden administration proposed to nearly double capital gains taxes for individuals earning more than $1 million to a staggering 39.6 percent. This would have been the highest percentage on investment earnings since the 1920s. Individuals generating more than $200,000 currently pay a capital gains rate of around 23.8 percent (including the 3.8 percent net investment tax) which helps fund the Affordable Care Act, otherwise known as Obamacare. Moreover, affluent Americans might have faced a federal capital gains tax rate of 43.4 percent under the proposed plan, including Obamacare tax. Additionally, when state taxes get factored in some Americans in New York and California would have paid a total capital gains tax rate of upwards of 50 percent or more. While legislation to raise taxes to these levels seems unlikely to pass at the time of this writing, it's just another example of how your assets and income are squarely in the government's crosshairs and why the type of planning we are discussing is so vitally important.

Estate Taxes

The desire to keep what you've earned and pass it on to your heirs without the tax collector or other outsiders filling their pockets is a common human desire. Taking steps to protect your wealth and assets and to control how they will be disbursed after your death is not a recent phenomenon. There is evidence of state tax planning in the form of a will that was used in Egypt more than three hundred years before Christ. The Romans implemented a legal instrument, much like our modern will, to control the dispersing of assets after the owner's death. Wills were used by the upper class in England before the Norman Conquest, but interest in controlling what happened to an individual's wealth and assets after death really soared after the Conquest. Today, to paraphrase legal professor and scholar William D. Rollison, there is no area of the law of more interest to Americans than that which applies to estate planning. (Side note: in an article published in the *Notre Dame Law Review,* Professor Rollison notes, "estate planning isnot, in modem law, a job for the amateur or the general practitioner — it is a task for the expert." I wholeheartedly agree with that assertion, and no, I'm not attempting humor.)

In the United States, estate tax became an official tax about a century ago. It was intended to take money from citizens with the deepest pockets to stimulate philanthropic efforts and maintain access to the wealth and power concentration throughout the nation. Thus, the first official estate tax emerged in the form of the Revenue Act of 1916. As previously stated, this act taxed the transfer of wealth from an estate to its beneficiaries. A core difference of this act from previous inheritance tax models was that the estate was levied instead of the individual beneficiaries. The tax due was calculated according to the estate's net worth, with an exemption of $40,000 for American residents. If non-residents owned or inherited American property, the exemption was not available to them. Under this act, taxes were due one year after the decedent's date of death. For any tax payments paid before the first year was up, the beneficiaries were entitled to a 5 percent discount on the amount due. However, a late payment incurred a penalty of 6 percent.

Estate Tax Attributes

The federal estate tax, often called the inheritance tax (or death tax as it was termed for propaganda purposes), is levied primarily on the estates of multimillionaires and billionaires before their assets are passed down to their heirs and/or descendants. There are a few different options for paying this tax, and there are exemptions that the government puts in place to keep those who are subject to the tax thriving, especially in the wake of the death of a family member. Nevertheless, putting a loved one to rest and then subsequently paying the government for your loss is hardly an appropriate condolence. Fortunately, the system that we provide will make this process a little easier for your loved ones, at least from a financial perspective.

Estate Tax Distinctions

Because the government, whether federal or state, has a proclivity to choose the most convoluted path more often than not, there is an ever-evolving system of rules for estate taxes. System? Actually, anything to do with estate taxes can be more like a labyrinth, and yes sometimes the IRS seems as ravenous as the Minotaur. And it's not just the IRS and federal tax code you need to worry about. In addition to your federal estate taxes, there are also estate taxes at the state level. Let's cover their distinctions.

Federal Estate Tax

The Internal Revenue Service mandates that estates with total gross assets and preceding taxable contributions of more than $12.06 million ($24.12 million for a married couple) must file a federal estate tax return for the tax year 2022 and settle the applicable estate tax. The percentage of the estate that exceeds $12.06 million will be levied at the highest federal statutory estate tax rate of 40 percent. However, professional tax accountants can use various discounts, deductions, and loopholes to reduce the effective tax rate significantly. One of these strategies is to take advantage of the estate's flexibility in terms of the valuation date to minimize the estate's value or cost base.

State Estate Tax

Some states impose their own estate taxes in addition to the estate taxes at the federal level. Individuals living (and dying) in one of these states are more likely to be affected by these estate taxes than by those who pay them at the federal level. State and district estate tax exemptions can go as low as $1,000,000 comparatively speaking. With that information in mind, below are the jurisdictions that impose estate taxes:

- Connecticut
- District of Columbia
- Hawaii
- Illinois
- Maine
- Maryland

- Massachusetts
- Minnesota
- New York
- Oregon
- Rhode Island
- Vermont
- Washington State

- New York
- Oregon
- Rhode Island
- Vermont
- Washington State

Above the limitations, the tax gets calculated frequently on a sliding scale, comparable to income tax levels. The tax rate is usually around 10 percent for amounts beyond the threshold and then climbs in increments, generally reaching 16 percent. The tax is the lowest in Connecticut where it starts at 10 percent and grows to 12 percent. The highest is in Washington State where it can reach 20 percent.

How the Estate Tax Exemption Works

Before estate taxes are due, the gross worth of an estate must exceed the exemption threshold during the year of death. Even then, only the portion of the value that exceeds the exemption is deemed taxable. For example, assume a person died in 2021 with a net worth of $21,580,000. Given the $11,580,000 estate tax exemption, the deceased's estate would be subject to a high federal estate tax rate of 40 percent on $10 million, or over $4 million. You would need to pay federal estate taxes on the first $1 million over the federal estate tax exemption threshold, which is $345,800. The remaining $9 million would be subject to a 40 percent marginal estate tax rate, bringing the total to $3.6 million. For an estate worth $10 million more than the federal estate tax exemption limit, federal estate taxes would then be: $3,600,000 + $345,800 = $3,945,800.

In 2022, the yearly gift tax exclusion threshold is $16,000. To put it another way, you could give $16,000 each year to an endless number of people without the gifts counting against your estate. Now, suppose you expect your estate to exceed the estate tax exemption threshold, or you know your estate is already well beyond the exemption level. In either of these cases, it may be preferable to give your heirs the maximum annual gift tax exclusion amount immediately to lower your tax bill.

Estate Taxes in the United States During the Last Decade Over the next ten years, the plan for the estate tax is to raise it nearly $225 billion. During President Obama's second term, he sought to take estate taxes back to 2009 rates with an individual exemption of $3.5 million for individuals, $7 million for couples, and a top tax rate of 45 percent. If all the tax reforms that Obama proposed had passed, the changes could very well have generated an additional $131 billion over the following ten years by affecting three estates out of every 1,000 deaths.

Estate tax reforms have been caught in a game of tug-of-war since the formation of the United States tax code. The cyclical nature of this activity makes it imperative that we look back to the most significant applicable legislation that has laid the foundation for present-day taxation.

Job Creation Act of 2010

Former President Barack Obama signed the Tax Relief, Unemployment Insurance Reauthorization, and Job Creation Act of 2010 on December 17, 2010. This act extended the Bush-era tax cuts until December 31, 2012. Additionally, federal estate and gift tax laws also changed dramatically. This law also set the federal estate and generation-skipping tax exemptions at $5 million per person, with a top tax rate of 35 percent. It permitted the executor of an estate to choose between paying zero federal estate tax on an adjusted carryover basis or to apply the $5 million exemption threshold with an indefinite step-up or increase. For example, assume a person died in 2021 with a net worth of $21,580,000. Given the $11,580,000 estate tax exemption, the deceased's estate would pay a high federal estate tax rate of 40 percent on $10 million, or over $4 million.

The legislation also unified the estate and gift tax exemptions until the end of 2012, capped them at $5 million, and imposed a 35 percent gift tax rate should the gift tax exemption be surpassed during an individual's lifetime. This unification meant the $5 million exemption could be spent during the individual's lifetime or at their death (or in any combination of these) without being negatively impacted. Furthermore, a $4 million increase was exacted over the previous gift tax exemption, unfolding a whole new world of estate planning for those with more extensive estates.

The law allowed unused estate tax exemptions to be transferred between spouses for the first time. Previously, if a taxpayer left all their assets and possessions to their spouse, the estate tax-exempt status was forfeited, prompting the widespread usage of what are known as credit shelter trusts. Whereas now, any unclaimed exemption can be handed on to the surviving spouse after death, giving the spouse a maximum exemption of $10 million.

American Taxpayer Relief Act (ATRA)

On January 1, 2013, Congress enacted the American Taxpayer Relief Act (ATRA). The following day, President Obama signed it into law. ATRA sought to establish permanent modifications to the laws that regulate federal estate taxes, gift taxes, and generation-skipping transfer taxes. The enactment of ATRA prevented most of the key tax cuts passed between 2001 and 2010 from expiring. For example, the Economic Growth and Tax Relief Reconciliation Act of 2001 and the Jobs and Growth Tax Relief Reconciliation Act of 2003 were made permanent upon ATRA'senactment into law. Additionally, the act extended the American Recovery and Reinvestment Act of 2009's tax cuts through2017.

Aside from the prolonged tax cuts, ATRA increased payroll taxes for manyAmericans and repealed tax cuts for the affluent Americans enacted during the Bush Administration. In addition, the White House sought to cut the deficit by $737 billion at that time.

Summary

As an affluent member of the top 1 percent, you should expect to be a prime target for taxation as federal spending swells, the deficit rises, and the government reaches for ways to collect more tax revenue. No one is fully impervious to losing their wealth. Since change is inevitable, and there is turnover even among the truly rich, it is important to understand proposed changes to taxation in the broader context of the history of estate and capital gains taxes.

A capital gains tax is imposed on the increase in the value of an investment when the gain is realized upon sale of the asset. Unsold investments or *unrealized capital gains* are exempt from taxation. Congress first gained the authority to impose income taxes in 1913. The first income tax was introduced that year, and it imposed a sevenfold higher rate of tax on the wealthy compared to mainstream Americans. The first capital gains tax was also introduced that same year. The benefit of capital gains taxes is that tax payments on an asset can be put off until it is sold. Since nearly everything an individual owns (whether it's personal in nature or an investment) is viewed as a capital asset by the IRS, and delayed taxes on capital gains confer advantages on the 1 percent. Yet, the capital gains tax rule has the disadvantage of reducing the overall earnings from an asset sale.

Capital gains tax rates can range from 0 percent to 20 percent depending on the taxpayer's tax bracket. Persons in the 10 percent and 15 percent tax brackets are not required to pay any long-term capital gains tax, whereas those in the 39.6 percent bracket pay the full 20 percent. In addition, most states require property owners and investors to pay taxes on capital gains from the sale of real estate. This double taxation further reduces the gain on the sale of a real estate. Capital losses from investments can offset taxes on capital gains.

There are exceptions to capital gains taxes, such as capital gains from the sale of collectibles and precious metals which fall under different regulations than other assets do. Capital gains regulations have changed numerous times. For instance, in 2020 the government set long-term capital gains tax rates at 0 percent, 15 percent, and 20 percent, depending on the taxpayer's income level.

Long-term capital gains have been taxable at lower rates than regular income for almost the entire history of income taxation. Qualified dividends have also been taxed at a lower rate since 2003. Yet current proposals on Capitol Hill are not designed to reduce taxes on the 1 percent. Under the changes proposed by the current administration, affluent Americans might be forced to pay a federal capital gains tax rate of 43.4 percent. Some Americans in New York and California may be required to pay state capital gains taxes as well, with a total capital gains tax rate of more than 50 percent.

Although the affluent are clearly viewed as taxation targets by legislators on Capitol Hill, the news from the federal government is not all negative. Estates that are vulnerable to the capital gains tax can benefit from certain exemptions. As we have discussed, to avoid the impact of a projected U.S. capital gains tax increase, most wealth planners advise clients to max out their retirement accounts, park their earnings in tax-deferred opportunity zone funds, and even liquidate some assets. Yet there is more that can be done. Over the course of four decades, my associates and I have created wealth preservation plans for thousands of our clients. The government does permit you to lower your tax burden significantly through trusts, tax-free accumulation products, and the types of strategies we have looked at throughout this book.

I will readily admit that this chapter covered a lot of material and some of the material would require even experts like me to put on our thinking caps. The idea of making it through the material may have seemed daunting when you started the chapter, so commendations are in order for sticking with me through it. Everything else from here on will be relatively smooth sailing.

Chapter 8

Don't Go It Alone: Working with Trusted Advisors

For those of you who stuck with me through the previous chapter as I regaled you with the history of estate planning and taxation since Ramses II was on the throne of Egypt, I commend your stamina, perseverance, and interest. Some people might find a discussion of legislation and history tedious, but it's to your advantage to understand as much as possible about anything involving taxes, economics, and history.

As you may also recall from the previous chapter (if you had the gumption to read through it all), I mentioned William D. Rollison, noted law professor, who believed firmly that estate planning was not something an individual should attempt alone. Professor Rollison pointed out that while the separate components of estate planning seem simple enough, putting together a plan to preserve and grow an estate is a complex endeavor made more difficult by the hidden pitfalls presented by the tax code. Failure to spot a pitfall could result in devastating losses. That's a chilling thought to imagine the financial rug being pulled out from underneath you, especially if you've been entertaining the idea of reducing your day-to-day involvement in your business or professional endeavors. I think we should consider Professor Rollison's wise words again: "[E]state planning is not, in modern law, a job for the amateur or the general practitioner; it is a task for the expert."

As I've mentioned earlier, my intention in writing this book was to share information so that you would have a better understanding of the shifting tax paradigm we face today, to suggest some investments that could be effective in estate planning, and perhaps to get you to view insurance in a different light. I want to stress that I didn't write this book as encouragement to turn estate planning into a do-it-yourself project. I agree wholeheartedly with Professor Rollison in that it would be grossly imprudent for an individual to dismiss expert advice and try to attempt to steer their own financial course. This book was intended to work in tandem with your trusted advisors, with an emphasis on the word *trusted.*

Choosing an advisor can be confusing. To begin with, there are numerous people (some with letters after their names) who possess varying degrees of education and knowledge regarding investments and estate planning. There are registered representatives, also known as stockbrokers, investment advisors, chartered financial analysts (CFA), personal financial specialists (PFS), and certified financial planners (CFP). Additionally, your accountant or banker or lawyer who is proficient in estate planning may be your choice to provide guidance on your estate planning.You need to pay close attention to the prospective advisor's education and experience as they apply to finance, investments, and estate planning. Learning that someone has been successfully working as a financial advisor for several decades tells you more about that person's qualifications than any number of certificates hanging on their office wall.

Today there are digital options for investment and estate planning that are known as robo-advisors. I'm not kidding. You can go online, fill out a form that solicits simple financial information, and receive a plan for investing that's based on a computer algorithm. As you might expect, the only advantage to using a robo-advisor is that it is very inexpensive. There's nothing personal about the service. If you learn of anyone contemplating using a robo-advisor, even a young person fresh out of college, remind that person that you get what you pay for. Advise them to save some money and consult an expert as soon as possible.

The more traditional route is to find an advisor with whom you can meet and who will guide you through the plethora of available financial options to find those best suited to your individual financial situation and your goals for the future. In addition to a potential advisor's education and experience, you should find out how the advisor plans to bill you. Some advisors charge by the hour for the time they spend both with you and for the time they spend working on your investments and estate planning. Some advisors work on commission which is usually based on a percentage of your investment fund they manage.

You also need to determine the standard of care to which that individual adheres. There are two: suitability and fiduciary. If the individual follows a suitability standard of care, they will offer products and plans that are suitable for someone in your position, even if they are not the best choices for your specific circumstances and goals. Stockbrokers often work to a suitability standard. However, someone who adheres to a fiduciary standard will work in the *client's* best interest regardless of their position. Adhering to a fiduciary standard means that the individual would revealany potential conflicts of interest and only suggest financial moves and strategies that would be in *your* best interest, not simply those that would be generally suitable to someone your age and with your net worth. As you can tell from this paragraph and my previous comments, my colleagues and I are firmly in the fiduciary camp. It's imperative for you to find someone who always has your best interests in mind and in whom you have complete confidence and trust. The following are a few traits you want your advisor to have:

- Your advisor should offer advice tailored to your specific circumstances and goals. You don't want some who tries to shoehorn you and your financial situation into a generic plan.

- Your advisor should listen to your concerns and respond with solid assurances, or they should mitigate or alleviate the source of the concern.
- Your advisor should have time for you. Now, you cannot expect anyone to be at your beck and call every minute of every day. You're not going to be your advisor's only client. However, when you have a question or need to adjust your estate plans because of life changes, you shouldn't need to wait weeks to speak to your advisor.
- You should feel you have a rapport with your advisor. You should feel confident that they understand where you want to go financially and what you want your investments working toward.
- If you don't feel comfortable with your current advisor, or you don't feel that they ever seem to have time for you or don't remember your goals, look for someone who will tick those boxes. Ideally you should have an advisor who has time for you, and whose advice is tailored specifically to your situation, your future prospects, and your goals. You want someone who keeps up with changes to applicable taxation laws/regulation and is up to date on available investment options.

Whether your advisor is your CPA or your trust and estate attorney or a certified financial planner, I think it is to your advantage to educate yourself about the various financial products available today. It is important to my colleagues and me that each of our clients are aware of the following strategies that are often used by your peers to help them control how their wealth is passed down to their heirs and how to limit the attendant tax bill. Like any of the other strategies out there, these strategies also have their pros and cons, so you want to take a close look before committing your funds. I feel strongly that it is vital that you understand the number of options you have at your disposal as we enter an unknown tax environment. There are plenty of solid options to choose from, and your trusted advisor should point you in the direction of the options that are the best fits for your situation and financial status.

The following options are some of the most touted by trust-and-estate professionals: GRAT, CRT, CLAT, and QPRT You may be no stranger to the alphabet soup of acronyms by which they are known because they are very popular among estate planning professionals. In fact, because they are so commonly bandied about, you may not have paid much attention to them. If that's the case, let me remedy that now with a concise description of how each option works.

> ***Authors Note: I would like to thank mypartner Paul Hyl, Esq. for his help and guidance reviewing the legal and technical aspects of this chapter. Paul is a noted trusts and estate attorney who is highly experienced at helping clients navigate through these often-confusing topics. His insight and knowledge helped me present these topics in an understandable*** *manner.*

Grantor Retained Annuity Trust (GRAT)

Agrantor retained annuity trust (GRAT) is created when a grantor contributes assets that have an appreciation potential to a fixed-term irrevocable trust. The grantor then retains the right to receive an annuity stream over the length of the trust's term. Once the term ends, the assets are distributed to noncharitable beneficiaries who are typically the grantor's children. The IRS subsequently assumes that the trust's assets will generate a return of at least the applicable Sec. 7520 rate which goes into effect the month that the assets are transferred to the trust. Any appreciation amount greater than the Sec. 7520 rate passes down to the beneficiaries and is not subject to gift tax. Should the assets within the GRAT fail to outperform the Sec. 7520 rate, then they would be returned to the grantor. At that point, the grantor would pay little to no gift tax, and would only incur minimal administrative costs for establishing and maintaining the GRAT. There are no other adverse tax consequences of a substandard-performing GRAT.

Let me illustrate one use of a GRAT.

Let's say an individual placed $5 million in a GRAT (an irrevocable trust that met the Sec. 2702 requirements) when the Sec. 7520 rate was 3.4 percent with the right to receive an annuity of $500,000 for ten years. At the end of ten years, the remainder would be distributed to the grantor's children. Using the IRS Publication 1457, "Annuities, Life Estates & Remainders," Table B factor of 8.3587, the annuity stream would be valued at $4,179,350, and the remainder interest would be valued at its then present value of $820,650. Now, if the assets appreciated at an Sec. 7520 rate of 3.4 percent, the grantor would then receive a stream of ten payments of $500,000. In addition, the beneficiaries would receive $1,146,484 at the end of the 10-year term (the future value of $5 million minus ten annual payments of $500,000 appreciating at 3.4 percent per year).

Now let's say the assets appreciated at a rate of 8 percent, but with the exact same payment structure. Then the beneficiaries would receive $3,551,344 (with a present value at 3.4 percent of $2,542,069). Only the then present value of the remainder interest (or $820,650) would be subject to the gift tax. Being that this was a gift of a future interest, it would still not be a completed gift and thus would not qualify for the annual gift tax exclusion. Any appreciation higher than this amount would transfer to the grantor's children free of gift tax consequences. In addition to the gift tax benefits, the value distributed to the beneficiaries would be removed from the grantor's estate. In contrast, the value of the annuity payments would remain in the grantor's estate. If the grantor died during the trust term, the value of the remainder interest would also be included in the grantor's estate. However, the grantor could pass the right to receive any remaining annuity payments to their surviving spouse, either outright orthrough a marital trust which would qualify them for the estate tax marital deduction and would eliminate any estate tax liability relating to the GRAT assets.

A properly structured GRAT treated as a grantor trust for principal and income purposes provides several advantages. First, all income, gains, losses, and credits are taxed to the grantor, but the grantor's income tax payments related to income from the GRAT are not treated as additional gifts to the trust. Because of this, the trust assets are not reduced by income taxes, thus resulting in a significantly higher residual payment to the beneficiaries. Second, a grantor trust can also be an S Corporation shareholder. Finally, any transactions between the grantor and the GRAT are ignored, so no gains or losses are recognized on any sales between the two.

Of course, like all things in life, there are some downsides to be considered. (There has been pressure in the past to increase the terms and overall effectiveness of GRATs. In 2011, GRATS came under fire from the Obama Administration, and legislation was proposed to require a minimum of ten years. This would have effectively made them an inadequate tool for passing down assets with minimal tax impact on heirs.) Some of the cons associated with GRATS are that the assets would need to appreciate faster than the Sec. 7520 rate over the term, and the grantor would need to live past the last payment in the term.

The GRAT would also need to perform for ten years, AND the grantor would need to outlive the term. Additionally, while the Sec. 7520 rate is currently low because of interest rates, this may not last as the Fed recently announced they will begin raising rates in 2023. Finally, the grantor would receive the right to an annuity stream and not the income of the trust. So, let's say the trust did not generate sufficient income. Then the trustee would need to dip into the principal in order to make the annuity payment. A taxable gift would be calculated by subtracting the value of the grantor's retained interest from the property's fair market value transferred to the trust.

Charitable Remainder Trust (CRT)

A charitable remainder trust (CRT) is an irrevocable trust that generates a potential income stream for you (the donor to the CRT) or other beneficiaries. The remainder of the donated assets then goes to your favorite charity or charities. In addition to generating income, this charitable-giving strategy enables you to pursue your philanthropic goals while simultaneously providing for living expenses. A charitable trust offers flexibility and some control over your charitable beneficiaries while offering lifetime income. That helps considerably with retirement, estate planning, and tax management.

A charitable remainder trust is also known as a *split-interest* giving vehicle. This allows you to make contributions to the trust while being eligible for a partial tax deduction. This would then be passed down to charitable beneficiaries based on the CRT's assets. A CRT allows you to name either yourself or someone else to receive a potential income stream for a set amount of years, but that stream can be no more than twenty years or for the life of one or more noncharitable beneficiaries. You can then name one or more charities to receive the remainder of the donated assets.

There are two main types of charitable remainder trusts: charitable remainder annuity trusts and charitable remainder unitrusts. Let's take a quick look at each type.

Charitable remainder annuity trusts (CRATs distribute a fixed annuity amount each year, but additional contributions are *not* allowed. Charitable remainder unitrusts (CRUTs) distribute a fixed percentage based on the balance of the trust assets (revalued annually), and additional contributions are permissible.

Contributions to CRATs and CRUTs are an irrevocable transfer of cash or property; both are required to distribute a portion of income or principal to either the donor or another beneficiary. The remaining trust assets are distributed to one or more charitable remainder beneficiaries at the end of the specified lifetime or term for the income interest.

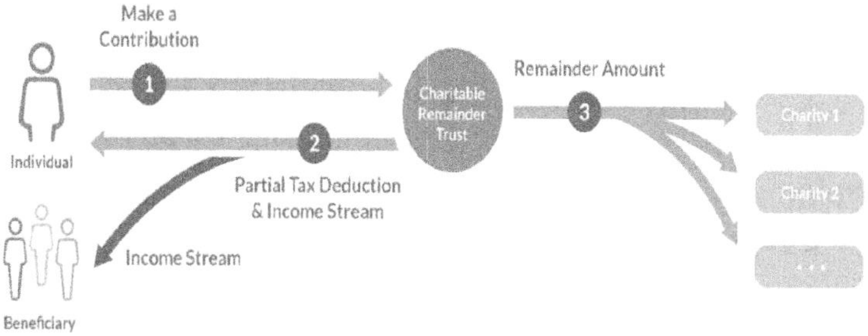

In the illustration above, you see Step 1 in which you would make a partially tax-deductible donation. For example, you could donate cash, stocks, or any non- publicly traded assets such as real estate, private business interests, orprivate company stock. This would make you eligible to take a partial tax deduction. The partial income tax deduction would be based on the type of trust, the term of the trust, and the projected income payments. The IRS interest rates would assume a certain rate of growth of the trust assets.

In Step 2, you or your chosen beneficiaries would receive an income stream. You could elect for the trust to pay income annually, semi-annually, quarterly, or monthly. Per the IRS: The annual annuity must be at least 5 percent, but no more than 50 percent of the trust's assets.

At Step 3, after the specified timespan or the death of the last income beneficiary, the remaining CRT assets would be distributed to the designated charitable beneficiaries. Upon termination of the CRT, the remaining CRT assets would be distributed to the charitable beneficiary which could be either public charities or private foundations. Depending on how the CRT was established, the trustee could have the power to change the CRT's charitable beneficiary during the lifetime of the trust.

There are several key benefits in establishing a CRT. The first is that you ultimately get to preserve the value of highly appreciated assets. This is especially relevant for those with significantly long-term appreciated assets including non-income producing property. A CRT allows you to contribute that property to the trust so that when the trust sells, it would then be exempt from tax. By donating the assets in kind to the CRT, the full, fair market value of the assets are preserved rather than reduced by hefty capital gains taxes. This allows more money for the income and charitable beneficiaries.

Income tax deductions are another appealing benefit associated with CRTs. Based on a calculation regarding the remainder distribution to the charitable beneficiary, income tax deductions enable you to take a partial income tax charitable deduction when you fund the trust.

Last but certainly not least, the CRT's investment income is exempt from tax which makes the CRT a fantastic option for asset diversification. Something to consider is donating low-basis assets toward the trust so that no income tax is generated to you when it sells, thus eliminating the capital gains tax on the sale of the asset. However, it should be noted that the named income beneficiary *will* pay income tax on the income stream received.

Even with all these positive aspects, you still need to consider the opposite side of the investment. You will need to make substantial contributions in order to provide income for yourself and value to the charity. These trusts are also irrevocable, so once they are finalized, you cannot alter any of their provisions should you have a change of heart. Furthermore, once these funds are placed into such a trust, you relinquish control over them. It also goes without saying that any income received from the charitable trust could potentially reduce the total contribution you end up leaving to your charity, and you may risk leaving nothing to your charity if you intend on receiving lucrative payments from the trust while you are still alive.

Charitable Lead Annuity Trust (CLAT)

You may not have heard of a charitable lead annuity trust (CLAT) even though this type of trust has been in use since the 1970s. Jacqueline Kennedy Onassis's will included a CLAT. This is a type of charitable trust that pays a charity, a donor-advised fund, or a foundation of the grantor's choice. Annual payments are either made for a set term of years or for the grantor's lifetime. At the end of this period, all remaining CLAT assets are distributed to the CLAT's non- charitable beneficiaries. This may be accomplished either by disbursements to the grantor's heirs or through continuing trusts for the benefit of those heirs. Establishing a CLAT enables grantors to provide a gift-tax-efficient way to transfer wealth to their heirs and contribute to their charitable beneficiaries.

Charitable Lead Annuity Trust (CLAT)

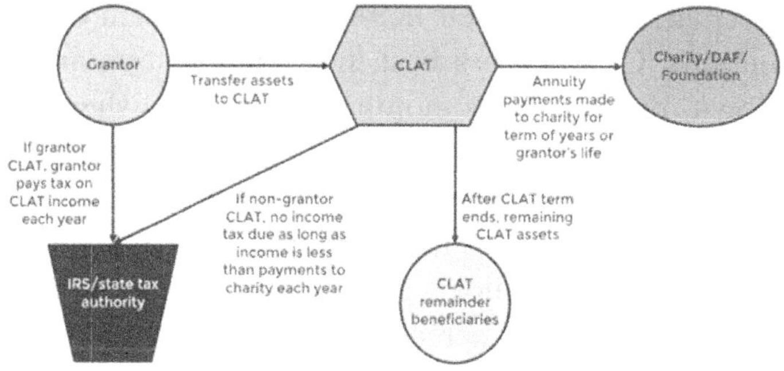

Let's take a look at how a CLAT works in order to better demonstrate its potential benefits to your estate planning. Let's assume Miss Jane contributed $1 million to a CLAT that lasted for ten years and paid 10.333 percent (or $103,330) annually to her favorite charity. With a 7520 rate of 0.6 percent, and assuming average growth of 15 percent annually of the CLAT assets, the result would be as follows:

Charitable Benefits: The charity received $1,033,300 ($103,330 annually for ten years) and a gift tax charitable deduction of $1million.

Wealth Transfer Benefits: Jane owed no gift tax and did not need to use any of her available gift tax exemption. At the end of ten years, the remaining CLAT assets, which would total $1,947,000, would be distributed amongst Jane's beneficiaries.

Income Tax Benefits: Assuming Jane's CLAT was structured so that she paid the taxes on the CLAT's income (a grantor CLAT), she would receive an immediate income tax charitable deduction of $1million to use starting with the tax year in which the CLAT was created and with a 5-year, carry-forward for any unused charitable deduction. Now, had Jane set it up so that the CLAT paid its own taxes, the CLAT itself would get an income tax charitable deduction each year equaling $103,330 per year, and Jane would receive no income tax charitable deduction.

A CLAT makes a lot of sense for high-net-worth individuals who desire to make charitable gifts while also transferring wealth to their heirs since it's absent of any gift exemptions. CLATs work best in low-interest environments and down markets. Each month, the IRS publishes a *hurdle* interest rate, which is called the 7520 rate; the lower the 7520 rate, the smaller the amount that must be paid to the lead beneficiaries. This leaves more value in the CLAT at the end of the term for the grantor's descendants. In December 2020, the 7520 rate was 0.6 percent. In November, the 7520 rate was 0.4 percent which was a record low. CLATs work well in a low-interest-rate environment because if the CLAT's growth exceeds the 7520 rate, this excess growth passes to the grantor's descendants free of gift tax obligations. The more undervalued the CLAT assets are at the time of funding, the more likely those CLAT assets will grow over the CLAT term when markets rebound. During the term, the more the CLAT growth exceeds the 7520 rate, the more wealth the CLATwill transfer to the next generation free of gift tax.

As I've quantified a few (okay numerous) times, there are usually downsides to just about everything, so let's look at the possible downsides to this investment. It's imperative to always consider the positives and negatives of any proposed investment. Unlike charitable remainder trusts, CLATs are not exempt from income tax. Suppose the grantor wants to claim the immediate income tax charitable deduction. In that case, the CLAT must be set up as a grantor trust so that all income generated by the CLAT during the trust term (even income distributed to the lead beneficiary) is taxable to the grantor. This is called a *Grantor* CLAT. The income tax charitable deduction equals the present value that the lead beneficiary's payments will receive over the term of the CLAT. A CLAT is a Grantor CLAT if the grantor or grantor's spouse retains a grantor-trust power such as the power to substitute trust assets with assets of equal value.

The extent to which a grantor may use the income tax charitable deduction in any particular year is limited to a portion of their total income for the year. This number can go as high as 30 percent should the CLAT be funded with appreciated assets, but only 20 percent of AGI if the lead beneficiary is a private foundation. The silver lining here is that the grantor can claim unused portions of the deduction in up to five additional carry-forward years in most cases.

Let's consider what would happen if the grantor obtained the income tax charitable deduction at the inception of the trust. In that case, the grantor would be required to report and pay tax on *all* CLAT income (even amounts paid to the lead beneficiary) in subsequent taxable years on the grantor's individual income tax return. Because the grantor benefited from the immediate income tax charitable deduction at the CLAT's inception, they would not receive any further income tax charitable deductions during the CLAT term for the future payments made to the lead beneficiary. If a grantor decided to turn off the grantor trust power, the CLAT would cease to be a grantor trust. The grantor would then be required torecapture a portion of the immediate income tax charitable deduction previously obtained. The grantor would also be required to include the recaptured CLAT income in their personal income tax return that year.

In addition, the lead beneficiary cannot be changed. However, backup lead beneficiaries can be named in the event the original lead beneficiary no longer qualifies as a charitable beneficiary. Also, the trustee may be given the discretion to pick the new lead beneficiary should the original no longer qualify. Furthermore, the grantor should not possess the power to change the lead beneficiary or decide how to apportion the annual payments amongst multiple lead beneficiaries. If they could, then the CLAT would be incorporated in the grantor's taxable estate upon death.

Qualified Personal Residence Trust (QPRT)

A qualified personal residence trust (QPRT) is a unique type of irrevocable trust that is designed to remove the value of your primary residence or second home from your taxable estate. A QPRT creates a legacy for your family and enables you to pass your residence on to your heirs in a manner that will encourage them to hold on to it for the long haul. This is an excellent option for anyone who wants their home to remain within their family for generations to come. A QRPT allows for continued use of the residence so that the homeowner can continue living there rent free and take all applicable income tax deductions during the retained income period of the QPRT.This retained income period is a time when the owner continues to live in residence before it transfers to a beneficiary.

The following types of trusts offer a few other significant financial perks as well. Let's dive into these treasure troves and find some additional gems of information.

As I mentioned, a QPRT removes the value of your primary or secondary residence from your taxable estate.

It also removes all future appreciation from your taxable

estate at cents on the dollar. Depending on interest rates, the homeowner's age, and the retained income period chosen for the QPRT, a homeowner can use as little as $100,000 of their lifetime gift tax exemption to remove a $500,000 asset from their taxable estate (assuming the home is worth $500,000). This is immensely beneficial if the house's value increases by a large margin at the time of the homeowner's death. A QRPT also hedges against potential decreases in the shared lifetime gift tax and estate tax exemption, otherwise referred to as the unified credit.

The lifetime exemption of $12.06 million in 2022 will let you establish a QPRT without having to pay any gift taxes. This is an important aspect to keep in mind when considering a QPRT since transferring your home to the trust is similar to gifting it to the trust, so gift taxes may potentially come knocking. The federal gift tax and federal estate tax share the $12.06 million unified credit. If you had devoted $5 million of the credit to gifts made during your lifetime, you would have $7.06 million remaining to apply to your estate. Should this shared exemption be reduced significantly at some point in the future, you would lock in the value of your residence for gift and estate tax purposes. Then you would not have to worry about how much the house might appreciate or what the estate tax exemption might be at the time of your death. If you were to die before the retained income period ends, then the QPRT transaction would be completely undone. The value of the residence would be included in your taxable estate at its full fair market value as of the date of your death.

There are other potential drawbacks to be considered as well. For example, ownership of the residence would pass to your heirs once the retained income period ended; this would eliminate your right to live in the residence rent free. Instead, you would be required to pay your heir's fair market rent if you wished to continue occupying the residence for an extended period. Heirs would inherit the residence with your income tax basis at the time the gift was made to the QPRT.

An heir who sold the home after the retained income period ended would owe capital gains taxes based on the difference between its cost basis and the sale price. Therefore, a QPRT is ideal for a residence that heirs plan to keep in the family for many generations.

Chapter 9

Summing It All Up

This book has been something of a roller-coaster ride, has it not? We have detailed the highs and lows of investing and taxation and have included a veritable alphabet soup of acronyms for investment options. We have covered a lot of ground. I'll bet that you were drawn to the book by the title, and when you began to read it, you expected a typical dry rendition of various methods of safeguarding your estate for the future. Instead, you found information on early attempts at estate planning that date back to the time of the pharaohs, an eye-opening look at life insurance (an innovative strategy known only to the most astute financial planners), lots of insider tips on how to choose an advisor, and investment vehicles that might be considered for your investment quiver. This book is full of good advice that could help you take your estate planning to the next level. Before I leave you, let me sum up some of the book's most important points.

Perhaps the most valuable piece of advice is to remember Professor William D. Rollison's assertion that financial planning is not something to be undertaken without the guidance of an expert. The laws and regulations that pertain to taxation aren't getting any less complex. If anything, they are becoming more intricate with each revision of the tax code, continually adding more places where you could be tripped up. Part of your advisor's job is to keep up with all changes in tax law as well as pertinent judicial interpretations of the tax code.

Don't take finding a financial advisor lightly. Use the points I provided to determine which advisor is best suited to you and your financial situation and goals. Ask friends and family for recommendations but remember that you want a professional, not a great tennis or golf partner. If you have a friend who sings the praises of an old college buddy (who is also their regular golfing partner), you shouldn't accept that seal of approval without close scrutiny of the proposed advisor. Everyone's financial situation and goals are different, and some people can tolerate more risk than others. As in any field, some advisors are meticulous in their work, and some are not. Do your homework and find the financial advisor who is right for you and with whom you feel comfortable. Remember that you get what you pay for so resist the temptation to go with someone because their fees are the lowest of the few advisors that you contacted. Engaging a financial advisor isn't something to do on a whim, certainly not when you're at a party having just met your neighbor's financial advisor. Take their card and check the individual's competency and experience out thoroughly. You need someone who you can trust and who will devise their suggestions and plans to best meet *your* financial goals.

The thing to keep in mind about taxes is that if you don't know the law and how it has been interpreted by the courts, you could find yourself lost in a dense forest without a clear path out. If you can keep abreast of proposed changes to the tax code, my hat is off to you. The tax code is intricate and complicated and relentlessly long. This is an area where you absolutely need the guidance of an experienced expert. You can explain to the IRS about how very sorry you are and how you thought you had complied, but you will still have to pay back taxes, fines, and interest if something was overlooked or reported incorrectly. Go ahead and listen to Uncle Morty as he regales the family with his brilliant tax-avoidance strategy; just don't follow his lead. Rely on your trusted advisor who has championed the ins and outs of tax law while taking the blind advice of friends or family with multiple grains of salt.

I know you were surprised when I touted the virtues and uses of poor old much-maligned life insurance, and I hope that after reading Chapter 2, you view life insurance in a completely different light. Life insurance may be a very efficient option for your estate, especially when structured in a cost-efficient manner as we reviewed. Seek the advice of your trusted advisor; consider whether it has a place in your wealth and assets preservation plan. It's worth remembering the old adage that you can't tell a book by its cover. You may think you know everything there is to know about life insurance or another aspect of financial planning, but perhaps you don't. Perhaps there are new ways to utilize the financial product that could greatly benefit your situation/circumstances. Don't dismiss something out of hand. Ask your financial advisor to explain the benefits and drawbacks of the financial product or strategy. Only after you thoroughly understand something (with your advisor's help) should you decide whether it is best for you.

I delved into strategies appropriate for the established affluent and then a different set of strategies appropriate for the mature affluent. The most significant point to take away from those discussions is that your approach must be appropriate for your stage of life. For the younger business owners and professionals who are at a time in their life when they are primarily seeking to build wealth aggressively, the tax efficiency of their strategies is a very important component of their planning blueprint. Generally, our younger affluent clients can tolerate more risk because they have more time to recover from any losses that their investments could incur. This allows the cyclical nature of economic changes to work to their advantage. Additionally, some strategies take longer to yield profitable results and are therefore not suitable for a mature investor. Asset allocation should be determined according to the investor's stage of life. For example, younger investors usually have more invested in the stockmarket than more mature investors. When utilizing the *Invest in Your Life* strategy, there are certain policies for which this is a key factor.

Typically, investors are willing to take on more risk until about ages fifty to sixty. Then they become more risk neutral or risk adverse and are principally interested in positioning their holdings so that they can weather the ups and downs of the economy and market without major shifts in value. These individuals, who I term the mature affluent, have accumulated wealth and assets through years of driving a business or professional practice to increasing prominence and prosperity. At this stage of life, they don't necessarily want to rest on their laurels. They want to ensure that the wealth and assets that they worked hard to build will be carefully preserved and protected from changes in the economy and tax laws. They want to rest assured that their estate will be disbursed according to their wishes. While working with an experienced advisor, they can formulate plans to ensure that their investments are positioned in the most advantageous way for their stage of life.

My discussion of how to use captive insurance to the benefit of your business (and ultimately your personal wealth) may well have taken you aback and initially seemed like a fairy tale. Now you know that owning your own insurance company is a valid and useful investment strategy utilized by none other than famed investor Warren Buffett. I hope that after reading Chapter 6 you give serious thought to the concept of captive insurance. I realize owning an insurance company isn't something you may have ever envisioned yourself doing, but as I pointed out, there are some distinct advantages to this strategy. If my discussion of the possibilities of captive insurance have piqued your interest and stirred questions, we would welcome a chance to elucidate the plan as it might apply to your situation. I'm proud of the hard work that went into devising the strategy and am pleased by the many clients we've helped benefit from it.

I hope that you have found this book to be both educational and enlightening. I also hope that you'verealized that certain strategies which you may have overlooked are actually worth your consideration. (Case in point: It's not your grandpa's life insurance anymore.) The information that I have shared in this book can help you no matter what your stage of life. Just keep in mind the tips I shared in Chapter 8 about finding a financial advisor who you can trust. No matter how well you think you've grasped a financial strategy, don't attempt to tackle, and implement a complicated, sophisticated, investment strategy on your own. We each have our area of expertise that we have built over years of experience, and it's a wise person who recognizes the benefits to be had from consulting someone whose expertise in an area exceeds their own.

The fact that you bought and read this book tells me that you have drive and determination. I would wager that you have found success in your chosen profession or line of business. You are building or have built your wealth and assets, and you are just as determined that they're not going to dwindle because of inattention. You want to preserve your estate and pass it on to your heirs. I understand and share your determination. To quote American businessman Robert Kiyosaki, "It's not how much money you make, but how much money you keep, how hard it works for you, and how many generations you keep it for." I couldn't have expressed that sentiment better myself. That is the ultimate goal that my colleagues and I strive to reach for each of our clients and ourselves.

Appendix A
United States 2020 Life Expectancy Table

Age	Female Life Expectancy	Male Life Expectancy
45	36.36	32.23
50	31.80	27.92
60	23.11	19.81
70	15.36	12.81
80	8.94	7.31

Appendix B

$10,000,000 Guaranteed Universal Life

Survivorship Life Preferred Rating

Year – Ages	Annual Premium	Death Benefit	IRR Death Benefit	Taxable Equivalent IRR Death Benefit*
1 – 70/70	$213,880	$10,000,000	4,575%	6,932%
5 – 75/75	$213,880	$10,000,000	86%	131%
10 – 80/80	$213,880	$10,000,000	27.04%	40.97%
20 – 90/90	$213,880	$10,000,000	7.54%	11.42%
30 – 100/100	$213,880	$10,000,000	2.73%	4.14%

**The Taxable Equivalent IRR reflects an assumed annual tax rate of 34%. These hypothetical returns are for demonstrative purposes only and do not represent any investments available in the market*

Appendix C

$10,000,000 Guaranteed Universal Life

Male Preferred Rating

Year – Age	Annual Premium	Death Benefit	IRR Death Benefit	Taxable Equivalent IRR Death Benefit*
1 - 70	$290,446	$10,000,000	3,432%	5,200%
5 - 75	$290,446	$10,000,000	73.10%	110.76%
10 - 80	$290,446	$10,000,000	21.73%	32.88%
20 - 90	$290,446	$10,000,000	4.93%	7.47%
30 - 100	$290,446	$10,000,000	0.87%	1.32%

**The Taxable Equivalent IRR reflects an assumed annual tax rate of 34%. These hypothetical returns are for demonstrative purposes only and do not represent any investments available in the market*

Appendix D

$10,000,000 Guaranteed Universal Life

Female Preferred Rating

Year – Age	Annual Premium	Death Benefit	IRR Death Benefit	Taxable Equivalent IRR Death Benefit*
1 - 70	$255,824	$10,000,000	3,808%	5,758%
5 - 75	$255,824	$10,000,000	78.68%	119.09%
10 - 80	$255,824	$10,000,000	23.93%	36.21%
20 - 90	$255,824	$10,000,000	6.02%	9.12%
30 - 100	$255,824	$10,000,000	1.66%	2.51%

**The Taxable Equivalent IRR reflects an assumed annual tax rate of 34%. These hypothetical returns are for demonstrative purposes only and do not represent any investments available in the market*

Ron has 30 years of detailed knowledge and earned experience in the insurance and wealth management industry. He has held management positions at the world's top insurance companies and helped grow a number of nationally recognized producer groups. His philosophy includes leveraging macro views of financial planning in order to develop specific wealth building and capital preservation strategies for clients. Ron is also an accomplished author, having penned a popular book, Invest In Your Life: Why Wall Street Wants You – an insider's look into the issues regarding the sale of life insurance policies to secondary investor groups. He has over the years also been a regular contributor to several nationally recognized industry publications, including The CPA Journal, The National Underwriter, and The Journal of Accountancy.

Ron received a B.A. from The George Washington University in 1988, and then went on to earn the industry-respected Chartered Life Underwriter and Chartered Financial Consultant designations from The American College in Bryn Mawr, PA. Ron also serves on the prestigious International Advisory Committee for EcoPeace Middle East – a unique organization that promotes peace in the Middle East based upon the common need for water and other natural resources. Ron resides in Upper Brookville, NY with his wife Claudia and his children Zachary & Hanna.

Made in the USA
Monee, IL
04 November 2026

67383008R10075